G Graphentis
  Verlag

International Journal for

Digital Art History

Editors
Dr. Harald Klinke
Ludwig Maximilian University
Munich, Germany

Liska Surkemper
Technical University
Munich, Germany

editors@dah-journal.org

Publisher
Graphentis Verlag e.K., Munich, Germany
www.graphentis.de

Issue 1/2015, June 2015
ISSN: 2363-5401 (online), ISSN: 2363-5398 (print)
www.dah-journal.org

Advisory Board
Dr. Anna Bentkowska-Kafel
King's College London, UK

Prof. Dr. Günther Görz
Friedrich-Alexander-Universität
Erlangen-Nürnberg, Germany

Prof. Dr. Hubertus Kohle
Ludwig Maximilian University
Munich, Germany

Dr. Maximilian Schich
University of Texas, USA

Disclaimer
The Publisher and Editors cannot be held responsible for errors or any consequences arising from the use of information contained in this journal. The views and opinions expressed do not necessarily reflect those of the Publisher and Editors, neither does the publication of advertisements constitute any endorsement by the Publisher and Editors of the products advertised.
Contributions are welcome. Please check our website for submission details: http://www.dah-journal.org. We accept no liability for unsolicited manuscripts and pictures. Authors agree to the terms and conditions and assure that the submission is free of third parties rights. The author grants a royalty-free and irrevocable right to freely publish documents submitted.

Copyright 2015 Graphentis Verlag e.K. All rights reserved. No part of this publication may be reproduced, stored or transmitted in any form or by any means without the prior permission in writing from the copyright holder.

Title image: Detail from image by Lev Manovich on page 16: a random sample of 50,000 Instagram images from Tokyo. (Source: Phototrails, http://phototrails.net/, 2013)

© Graphentis Verlag, Munich 2015

ISBN 978-3-942819-10-7

ISSN: 2363-5398 (print version)
ISSN: 2363-5401 (electronic version)

Contents

Editorial 6

Featured Article

Lev Manovich
Data Science and Digital Art History 12

What is Digital Art History?

Benjamin Zweig
Forgotten Genealogies: Brief Reflections on the History of Digital Art History 38

Anna Bentkowska-Kafel
Debating Digital Art History 50

Elli Doulkaridou
Reframing Art History 66

Interview

Park Doing and C. Richard Johnson, Jr.
On Applying Signal Processing to Computational Art History: an Interview 86

Quantitative Approaches

K. Bender
Distant Viewing in Art History. A Case Study of Artistic Productivity 100

Javier de la Rosa and Juan-Luis Suárez
A Quantitative Approach to Beauty. Perceived Attractiveness of Human Faces in World Painting 112

Call for Manuscripts #2 131

Editorial

Harald Klinke, Liska Surkemper

The digital age has revolutionized many spheres of the modern world: society as a whole, the economy as well as our private lives. Financial transactions happen in real time, global communication via the Internet is available free of charge, and the smartphone is our ubiquitous companion. Moreover, the natural sciences have enjoyed tremendous success from using new technology. The vast amount of data contained within the human genome could only be unlocked with the help of computers. And Big Data Analysis has turned into a new method for discovering otherwise hidden structures.

None of that has gone unnoticed in the Humanities. For decades now, the so-called digital humanities have striven to use algorithms to attain their objectives. Robert Busa started with his machine-generated concordance back in 1951, and text mining has since developed into an established method in literary studies. And art history?

Some say that except for using a word processor not much has changed in art history. We have digitized the slide library, but the image database very much still resembles its physical model in function. Can't we imagine much more? Certainly, we can do more with the image database alone. The fact that our art historical data is digital opens up a whole universe of possibilities. And the use of computers will revolutionize our discipline in many ways. The truth is: the future is already here. Research fields and methods have already changed. Digital art history has existed in many ways for a couple of decades. Publications, conferences and Summer Schools on the topic have been organized and many digital projects are popping up all over the world. What has been missing is a means of bringing concepts and projects to an audience of digital art historians who are scattered all over the world and engaging them in a fruitful discourse. What has been missing is a platform for exchange and networking.

The fact that our art historical data is digital opens up a whole universe of possibilities

The *International Journal for Digital Art History* (DAH-Journal) provides the opportunity to reflect on changes currently happening and thus make it possible to discuss questions concerning the future of our discipline, for example: what will art history look like in 5 or 10 years? Will art historians become data analysts? How do digital methods alter our traditional objectives? What is our relation to computer science? How do we adapt university curricula to this change?

When the strongest call to action around researchers in the digital humanities is to "Get data!" in order to get things started, perhaps it is also the time to ask: what kind of data do we *really* need and for what purpose? Collecting art-historical data is still time consuming, and one has to analyze it, develop algorithms for it and so on. Thus one task of this journal is to report which data sets already exist and are in use, and point out where gaps remain – and discuss which should actually be filled in order to get useful results.

Eventually, we as a community will have to decide which way we want to go with technology. We want to take part in developing and strengthening collaborative work internationally and interdisciplinarily and – amongst other things – bringing art historians and computer scientists together.

Art history has never been afraid of new technology. Think of Heinrich Wölfflin's use of slide projection 100 years ago. He changed the method of art history for good. A professor at the Ludwig Maximilian University of Munich, he was one of the first to regularly use slide projectors in his lectures. Using two projectors at the same time, he was able to compare two art works simultaneously. This fact and the rest of his academic career are well known history. His scientific achievements were a game changer in perceiving, analyzing and presenting works of art in the scientific world and beyond.

> *Eventually, we as a community will have to decide which way we want to go with technology*

Today, being in the middle of an even larger and broader paradigm shift – the digital revolution – art historians face particular challenges in contrast to other disciplines in the digital humanities. Because we primarily work with pictures rather than texts, we have to deal with issues of computer vision, reproduction quality, copyright issues, and so on. Therefor the DAH-Journal addresses these problems and informs the community of current projects and progress in the field. That the home base of the journal is in Munich, where Wölfflin once introduced a new technology in his lectures, could be a random fact. However, we like to see it as a good omen.

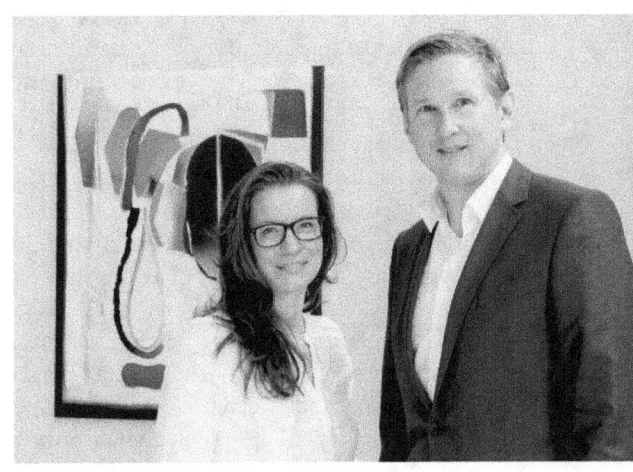

Liska Surkemper, Harald Klinke
(Photo: Janusch Tschech. Artwork „Nachschub": Li-Wen Kuo)

Editorial

In time the scientific approach, which we today call *digital art history*, will soon be just called *art history*. Again looking back in time, 100 years ago, nobody back then – even those against using new technologies – felt the need to label the approaches of Wöllflin, Warburg and others e.g. *mechanical art history*. One reason might be that it seemed obvious that the epistemic outcomes were still generated by humans and not by the technology – photography or slide projectors. Hence, we emphasize that art historians in their profession as scientists will *not* become obsolete – even if there are some prominent voices who foresee "The End of Theory" and with that the end of science as we know it, as Chris Anderson, publisher of *Wired* magazine, states in his eponymously titled article (Anderson 2008).

The word *digital* in the title of our journal points out that right now, as scientists still try to grasp all the pros and cons of the use of technology, it is of the utmost importance to reflect on and not to blindly applaud every development that is taking place. Beginning in this first issue by examining the fundamental question "What is Digital Art History?", we will dig into its history and present some intriguing results.

The journal is itself an experiment in publishing. As scholarly discours should be freely available, we have decided to publish open access. Since digital questions should be in the digital realm but the physical object remains important in the digital age, we publish online and in print. And believing e-publishing is more than a PDF-file on a web-server, we are probing what scholarly publishing can be and are open to new formats that meet the needs of the Humanities in the digital age. Accordingly, we will be constantly working on evolving our e-publishing format. We invite authors to write on new approaches to publishing work in the digital humanities community and we welcome critique as well as suggestions that help make this journal a worthy representative of our field.

The DAH-journal is already a success. The first tweet announcing the Call for Manuscripts was retweeted 76 times yielding a reach of tens of thousands and gaining 7,800 visits to the website. The interest in this topic is very strong and – we trust – will continue to be.

We would like to thank those people and institutions who have supported us thus far: our advisory board members, the reviewers, the Technical University of Munich and Ludwig Maximilian University, and of course the authors.

We would like to invite everyone to actively participate in the discourse on the future of art history as readers and authors. Hence, we would also like to draw your attention to page 131, where we have published the Call for Manuscripts for the second issue – please, spread the word! This journal is a platform for projects and ideas, for networking, expanding knowledge and pushing forward our discipline, art history.

United States	31,09 %
Germany	17,55 %
unknown	6,65 %
France	4,73 %
United Kingdom	4,16 %
Brazil	2,89 %
Russia	2,51 %
Canada	2,38 %
Italy	1,80 %
China	1,67 %

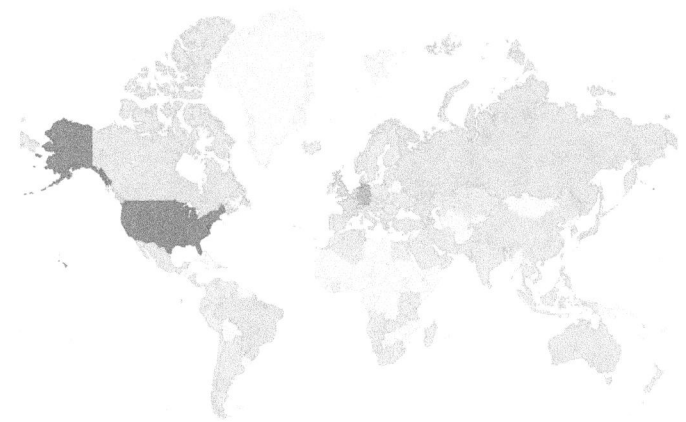

DAH-Journal's website analytics show visitors from all over the world (June 2015)

Harald Klinke has a Ph.D. in art history and a Master of Science in Information Systems. Currently he is Assistant Professor at the Ludwig Maximilian University, Munich, and responsible for the doctoral program "Digital Art History". He conducts research on visual communication, digital media, and Big Image Data in art-historical contexts.
From 2008 to 2009, he worked as a Lecturer of Visual Studies (Bildwissenschaft) at the Art History Department of the University of Göttingen. From 2009 to 2010, he conducted research, supported by a grant from the German Research Foundation (DFG), as a Visiting Scholar at Columbia University, New York. He has published books on American history paintings, digital images and art theory as visual epistemology.

Correspondence e-mail: h.klinke@lmu.de

Liska Surkemper is Associate Researcher for architectural and cultural theory at the Technical University Munich. She conducts research on visual epistemology and the interrelationship of pictures, architecture and economy.
From 2010 to 2014, she was a researcher and lecturer at the Department of Art Research and Media Philosophy at the University of Arts and Design Karlsruhe. She was also coordinator for the project "Memory of Scientific Knowledge and Artistic Approaches", which was supported by the German Federal Ministry of Education and Research (BMBF). Together with computer scientists, designers and arts scholars she helped develop the web application "Presenter" (http://presenter.hfg-karlsruhe.de): a tool for visualizing, sharing and archiving scientific and artistic knowledge.

Correspondence e-mail: liska.surkemper@tum.de

Featured Article

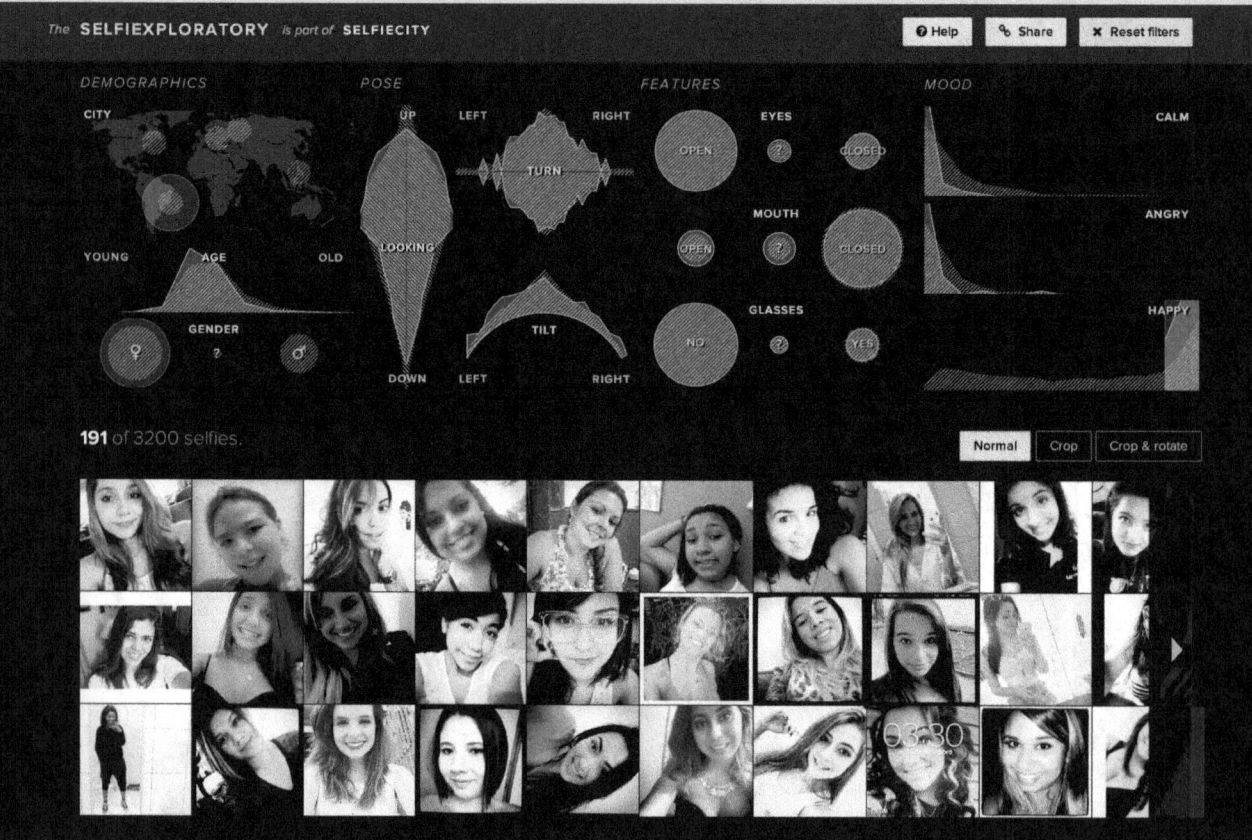

Figure 1: An example of the web interface for interactive exploration of image collections from our project *Selfiecity* (http://selfiecity.net, 2014).
A visitor can filter the collection of 3200 Instagram self-portraits by using graphs in the upper part of the screen. The left column contains graphs and controls for filtering images using cities, ages, and gender information. Age and gender estimates were obtained by using Amazon Mechanical Turk service. Other columns contain graphs that show features extracted by face analysis software from https://rekognition.com/.
They include face orientation (up/down, left/right, and degree of tilt), presence of smile and glasses, open/close eyes and mouth and seven emotions detected in faces (only three emotion graphs are included).

Invited Article
Data Science and Digital Art History

Lev Manovich

Abstract: I present a number of core concepts from data science that are relevant to digital art history and the use of quantitative methods to study any cultural artifacts or processes in general. These concepts are objects, features, data, feature space, and dimension reduction. These concepts enable computational exploration of both large and small visual cultural data. We can analyze relations between works on a single artist, many artists, all digitized production from a whole historical period, holdings in museum collections, collection metadata, or writings about art. The same concepts allow us to study contemporary vernacular visual media using massive social media content. (In our lab, we analyzed works by van Gogh, Mondrian, and Rothko, 6000 paintings by French Impressionists, 20,000 photographs from MoMA photography collection, one million manga pages from manga books, one million artworks of contemporary non-professional artists, and over 13 million Instagram images from 16 global cities.) While data science techniques do not replace other art historical methods, they allow us to see familiar art historical material in new ways, and also to study contemporary digital visual culture.

In addition to their relevance to art history and digital humanities, the concepts are also important by themselves. Anybody who wants to understand how our society "thinks with data" needs to understand these concepts. They are used in tens of thousands of quantitative studies of cultural patterns in social media carried out by computer scientists in the last few years. More generally, these concepts are behind data mining, predictive analytics and machine learning, and their numerous industry applications. In fact, they are as central to our "big data society" as other older cultural techniques we use to represent and reason about the world and each other – natural languages, material technologies for preserving and accessing information (paper, printing, digital media, etc.), counting, calculus, or lens-based photo and video imaging. In short, these concepts form the data society's "mind" – the particular ways of encountering, understanding, and acting on the world and the humans specific to our era.

Keywords: data science, data mining, visualization, data analysis, features, metadata, social media, algorithm, dataset

Introduction[1]

Will art history fully adapt quantitative and computational techniques as part of its methodology? While the use of computational analysis in literary studies and history has been growing slowly but systematically during 2000s and first part of 2010s, this has not yet happened in the fields that deal with the visual (art history, visual culture, film, and media studies).

However, looking at the history of adoption of quantitative methods in the academy suggests that these fields sooner or later will also go through their own "quantitative turns." Writing in 2001, Adrian Raftery points out that psychology was the first to adopt quantitative statistical methods in 1920s-1930s, followed by economics in 1930s-1940s, sociology in 1960s, and political science in 1990s.[2] Now, in 2015, we also know that humanities fields dealing with texts and spatial information (i.e., already mentioned literary studies and history) are going through this process in 2000s-2010s. So I expect that "humanities of the visual" will be the next to befriend numbers.

This adaption will not, however, simply mean figuring out what be counted, and then using classical statistical methods (developed by the 1930s and still taught today to countless undergraduate and graduate students pretty much in the same way) to analyze these numbers. Instead, it will take place in the context of a fundamental social and cultural development of the early 21st century – the rise of "big data," and a new set of methods, conventions, and skills that came to be called "data science." Data science includes classical statistical techniques from the 19th and early 20th century, additional techniques and concepts for data analysis that were developed starting in 1960s with the help of computers, and concepts from a number fields that also develop in the second part of the 20th century around computers: pattern recognition, information retrieval, artificial intelligence, computer science, machine learning, information visualization, data mining. Although the term "data science" is quite recent, it is quite useful as it acts as an umbrella for currently most frequently used methods of computational data analysis. (Alternatively, I could have chosen machine learning or data mining as the key term for this article, but since data science includes their methods, I decided that if I am to refer to all computational data analysis using a single term, data science is best right now.)

Data science includes many ideas developed over many decades, and hundreds of algorithms. This sounds like a lot, and it is. It is much more than can be learned in one or two graduate methods classes, or summarized in a single article, or presented in a single textbook. But rather than simply picking particular algorithms and techniques from a large arsenal of data science, or borrowing whatever technique happens to be the newest and therefore is currently in fashion (for example, "topic modeling" or "deep learning") and trying to apply them to art history, it is more essential to first understand the most fundamental assumption of the field as a whole. That is, we in art history (or any other humanities field) need to learn the core concepts that underlie the use of data science in contemporary societies. These concepts do not require formulas to explain, and they can be presented in one article, which is what I will attempt here. (Once we define these core concepts, a variety of terms employed in data science today can also become less confusing for the novice.)

Surprisingly, after reading thousands of articles and various textbooks over the last eight years, I have not found any short text that presents these core concepts together in one place. While many data science textbooks, of course, do talk about them, their presentation often takes place in the context of mathematically sophisticated techniques or particular applications which can make it hard to understand the generality of these ideas.[3] These textbooks in general can be challenging to read without computer science background.

Since my article is written for a humanities audience, it is on purpose biased – my examples of the application of the core concepts of data science come from humanities as opposed to economics or sociology. And along with an exposition, I also have an argument. I will suggest that some parts of data science are more relevant to humanities research than others, and therefore beginning "quantitative humanists" should focus on learning and practicing these techniques first.

From World to Data

If we want to use data science to "understand" some phenomenon (i.e., something outside of a computer), how do we start? Like other approaches that work on data such as classical statistics and data visualization, data science starts with representing some phenomenon or a process in a particular way. This representation may include numbers, categories, digitized texts, images, audio, spatial locations, or connections between elements (i.e., network relations). Only after such a representation is constructed, we can use computers to work on it.

In most general terms, creating such a representation involves making three crucial decisions:

What are the boundaries of this phenomenon? For example, if we are interested to study "contemporary societies," how can we make this manageable? Or, if we want to study "modern art," how we will choose what time period(s), countries, artist(s), and artworks, or other information to include? In another example, let's say that we are interested in contemporary "amateur photography." Shall we focus on studying particular groups on Flickr that contain contributions of people who identify themselves as amateur or semi-pro photographers, or shall we sample widely from all of Flickr, Instagram, or other media sharing service

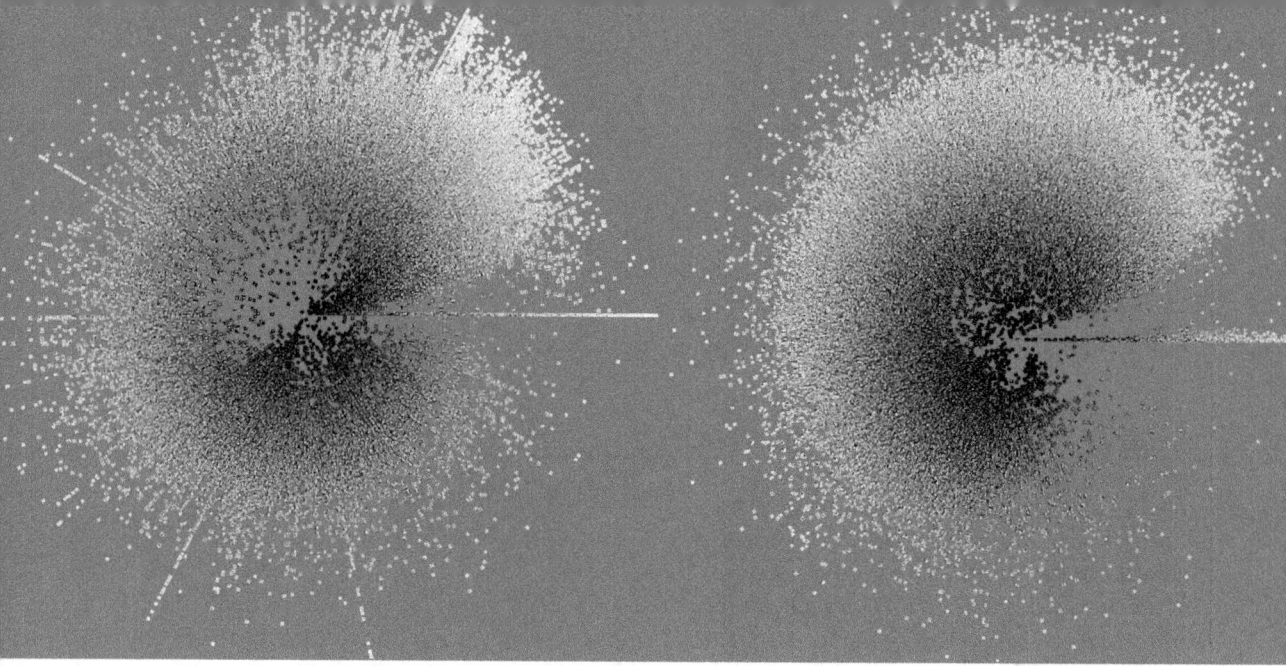

Figure 2: An example of visualizations of image collections that uses image features automatically extracted by a computer. (Source: our project Phototrails, http://phototrails.net/, 2013). Left: a random sample of 50,000 Instagram images from Bangkok. Right: a random sample of 50,000 Instagram images from Tokyo. In each visualization, images are organized by mean hue (angle) and brightness mean (distance to the center).

- since everybody today with a mobile phone with a built-in camera automatically becomes a photographer.

What are the objects we will represent? For example, in modern art example, we may include the following "objects" (in data science they can be also called data points, records, samples, measurements, etc.): individual artists, individual artworks, correspondence between artists, reviews in art journals, passages in art book, auction prices. (For example, 2012 *Inventing Abstraction* exhibition in MoMA in NYC featured a network visualization showing connections between artists based on the number of letters they exchanged.[4] In this representation, modernist abstract art was represented by a set of connections between artists, rather than any other kind of object I listed above.) In a "society" example, we can for instance choose a large set of randomly chosen people, and study social media they share, their demographic and economic characteristics, their connections to each other, and biological daily patterns as recorded by sensors they wear. If we want to understand patterns of work in a hospital, we may use as elements people (doctors, nurses, patients, and any others), also medical procedures to be performed, tests to be made, written documentation and medical images produced, etc.

What characteristics of each object we will include? (These are also referred to as metadata, features, properties, or attributes.). In humanities, we usually refer to characteristics that are already available as part of the data (because somebody already recorded them) and characteristics we have added (for example, by tagging) as metadata. In social science, the process of manually adding descriptions of data is called coding. In data science, people typically use algorithms to automatically extract additional characteristics from the objects, and they are referred as features (this process is called "feature extraction"). For example, artists' names is an example of metadata; average brightness and saturation of their paintings, or the length of words used in all titles of their works are examples of features that can be extracted by a computer. Typically features are numerical descriptions (whole or fractional numbers) but they can also take other form. For example, a computer can analyze an image and generate a few words describing content of the image. In general, both metadata and features can use various data types: numbers, categories, free text, network relations, spatial coordinates, dates, times, and so on.

Fig. 1 shows the examples of metadata and features used in one of the projects of my lab. We assembled a collection of 3200 Instagram self-portraits and created an interactive web interface for exploration of this collection. The examples of metadata are the same of the cities where Instagram images were shared. The features include estimate of the people age and gender, and results of computer analysis (emotions, face position and orientation, presence and amount of smile, etc.)

Fig. 2 shows examples of visualizations that present large image collections using features. 50,000 Instagram images shared in Bangkok are compared with 50,000 Instagram images shared in Tokyo using two features extracted by computer analysis – average color saturation, and average hue.

I suggest that in digital art history we adapt the term "features" to refer to both information that can be extracted from objects through computer analysis and the already available metadata. In natural and social sciences, the most common term is "variable," and it is used in the context of experiments. But since in humanities we do not do systematic experiments like in the sciences, for us the term "features" is better. It only implies that we represent objects by their various characteristics - but it does not imply any particular methods of analysis. (However, in the section "Classical Statistics and Statistical Graphs" below I will use "variable" because this was the term used during the period described in this section.)

Although it is logical to think of the three questions above as three stages in the process of creating a data representation – limiting the scope, choosing objects, and choosing their characteristics – it is not necessary to proceed in such linear order. At any point in the research, we can add new objects, new types of objects and new characteristics. Or we can find that characteristics we wanted to use are not practical to obtain, so we have to abandon our plans and try to work with other characteristics. In short, the processes of generating a representation and using computer techniques to work on it can proceed in parallel and drive each other.

Depending on our perspective, we could assume that a phenomenon (such as "contemporary society," for example) objectively exists regardless of how we study it (i.e., what we use as objects and their properties). Or we can also assume that a phenomenon is equal to a set of objects and their properties used in different qualitative and quantitative studies, publications and communication about it (books, articles, popular media, academic papers, etc.) That is, a phenomenon is constituted by its representations and the conversations about it. My description of the three questions above assumes the first position, but this is done only for the convenience of explaining the steps in moving "from world to data."

Objects + Features = Data

Together, a set of objects and their features constitutes the "data" (or "dataset").

People in digital humanities always like to remind us that data is something that is "constructed" – it does not just exist out there. But what does this mean exactly? Any data project, publication, or data visualization includes some aspects of the phenomena and excludes others. So it is always "biased." But this is something that in most cases can be corrected. For example, in the case of a survey of social media use that only samples people in the U.S. and asks them particular questions about their social media use (such as popular Pew Internet surveys), we can add people from different countries and we can also ask them additional questions. But the concept of "data" also contains more basic and fundamental assumptions that cannot be changed, and this is equally important. Before we can use computers to analyze a phenomena or activity, it has to be represented as a finite set of individual objects and also a finite set of their features. For example, consider music. The computational analysis of music typically divides a music track into very small intervals such as 100 ms and measures some properties of each sample. In this way, analog media is turned into discrete data.

How is a "data representation" of some phenomenon today different from other kinds of cultural representations humans used until now, be they representational paintings, literary narratives, historical accounts, or hand drawn maps? Firstly, a data representation is modular, i.e. it consists from separate elements: objects and their features. Secondly, the features are encoded in such a way that we calculate on them. This means that the features can take a number of forms – integers, floating point numbers, categories represented as integers or text labels, etc. – but not just any form. And only one format can be used for each feature.

But the most crucial and interesting difference, in my view, is that a data representation has two types of "things" which are clearly separated: objects and their features. What is chosen as objects, what features are chosen, and how these features are encoded – these three decisions are equally important for representing phenomena as data – and consequently, making them computable, manageable and knowable though data science techniques.

Practically, objects and features can be organized in various ways, but the single most common one is a familiar table. An Excel spreadsheet containing one worksheet is an example of a table. A table can be also stored as a standard text file if we separate the cells by some characters, such as tabs or commas (these are stored as .txt or .csv files, respectively). A relational database is a number of tables connected together though shared elements.

A table has rows and columns. Most frequently, each row is reserved to represent one object; the columns are used to represent the features of the objects. This is the most frequent representation of data today, used in every professional field, all natural and social science, and in government services. It is the way data society understands phenomena and individual, and acts on them.

Classical Statistics and Modern Data Science: From One to Many Variables

Classical Statistics and Statistical Graphs: Dealing with One or Two Variables

Statistics comes from the word "state," and its rise in the 18th and 19th century is inseparable from the formation of modern bureaucratic, "panopticon" societies concerned with counting, knowing and controlling its human subjects, and also its economic resources. Only in the middle of the 19th century, the meaning of "statistics" changes – it becomes a name for an independent discipline concerned with producing summaries and reasoning about any collections of numbers, as opposed to only numbers important for the states and industry.

For our purposes – understanding core principles of contemporary data science and how they are different from classical statistics – we can divide the history of statistics in three stages. The first stage encompasses 18th and first part of the 19th century. During this stage, statistics means collecting and tabulating various social and economic data. During this stage, William Playfair and others develop a number of graphing techniques to represent such collections visually. Playfair is credited with introducing four fundamental techniques: bar chart and line graph (1786), and pie chart and circle graph (1801). The titles of the books where Playfair first used these techniques exemplify the kinds of number gathering that motivated the invention of these techniques: *The Commercial and Political Atlas: Representing, by Means of Stained Copper-Plate Charts, the Progress of the Commerce, Revenues, Expenditure and Debts of England during the Whole of the Eighteenth Century* (1786); *Statistical Breviary; Shewing, on a Principle Entirely New, the Resources of Every State and Kingdom in Europe* (1801).

These graphing techniques invented by Playfair are still most popular today, despite the invention of other data visualization techniques in later periods. Note that they all visualize only a single characteristic of objects under study. Built into all statistical and graphing software and web services, they continue to shape how people use and think about data today – even though computers can do so much more!

(Note: When you make a graph in a program such as Excel, you often also select an extra column that contains labels. So even though these techniques show only patterns in a single characteristic – i.e., some numbers stored in a single column – in order to include the labels for the rows, a second column is also used. But it is not counted as a data variable.)

In the 19th century topical maps also became popular. An example is a map of a country where the brightness of each part represents some statistics, such as literacy rate, crime rate, etc.[5] Although such maps are two-dimensional graphical representation, they still only use a single variable (i.e. a quantity is used to determine the brightness or graphic style for each part of the territory shown on a map).

In the second stage of statistics history (1830s-1890s), the analytical and graphical techniques are developed to study the relations between two characteristics of objects (i.e., two variables). In 1880s Francis Galton introduces concepts of correlation and regression. Galton was also probably the first to use a technique that we now know as a scatterplot. Today scatterplot remain the most popular techniques for graphing two variables together.[6]

One of the most famous uses of statistics in the 19th century exemplifies "data imagination" of that period. In 1830s Belgian Adolphe Quetelet measured height and weight in a large number of children and adults in different ages and published his results in a book that was to become famous: *A Treatise on Man and the development of his aptitudes* (1835). Quetelet concluded that these characteristics measured in large numbers of people follow a bell-like curve (called now Gaussian or normal distribution). Along with analyzing height and weight as single separate variables, Quetelet also analyzed their relations in many people, creating in 1832 the modern "body mass index." He found that, on the average, "the weight increases as the square of the height."[7]

More canonical examples can be found in the book considered to be the founding text of sociology – *Suicide* by Émile Durkheim (1897).[8] The book has dozens of data tables. Durkheim used such summary statistics to compare suicide rates in different population groups (Protestants vs. Catholics, single vs. married, soldiers vs. civilians, etc.). He then proposed theoretical explanations for these differences. (Note that the book does not have a single statistical graph, not any statistical tests of the significance of the differences.)

In the third stage (1900-1930) the statistical concepts and methods for the analysis of one or two variables were further refined, extended, systematized, and given rigorous mathematical foundation. These include summarizing a collection of numbers (measures of central tendency such as mean and median, and measures of dispersion, such as variance and standard deviation), analyzing relations between two variables (correlation and regression), doing statistical tests, and designing experiments that gather data to be analyzed with statistics. The key work in this period was done by Karl Pearson, Charles Spearman, Ronald Fisher working in England and the American Charles Pierce.[9]

The content of contemporary introductory textbooks on statistics for college students is very similar to the content of Fisher's book *Statistical Methods for Research Workers* published in 1925 – and we may wonder why we keep using the concepts and tools developed *before* computers to analyze "big data" today. The practicality of manual computation was an important consideration for the people who were consolidating statistics in the beginning of the 20th century. This consideration played key role in shaping the discipline, and consequently still forms the "imaginary" of our data society.

Modern Data Science: Analyzing Many Features Together

In the 20th century, statistics gradually develop methods for the analysis of many variables together (i.e., "multi-variable analysis"). The use of digital computers for data analysis after WWII facilitates this development. As computers get faster, analyzing more and more features together becomes more practical. By the early 21st century, a representation of phenomena that has hundreds or thousands of features has become commonplace. The assumption that objects are described using a large number of features is standard in data science, and this is one of its differences from classical early statistics.

While basic statistical classes today still focus on the techniques for the analysis of one or two variables, data science always deals with many features. Why? In social sciences, the goal is explanation, and its ideal method is systematic experiments. The goal of experiments is studying how some conditions may be affecting some characteristics of a phenomenon or activity. For example, how does a person's background (place of birth, ethnicity, education, etc.) affect her current position and salary? How does an athlete's preparation and diet affect her performance in multiple sports competition? If there are many factors and effects, it is not easy to understand what is affecting what. Therefore, in an ideal 20th century experiment, a researcher wanted to only measure one condition and one effect. All other factors ideally are held constant. In an experiment, one condition (called independent variable) is systematically changed, and the values of a single characteristics thought to be affected by this condition (called dependent variable) are recorded. After the experiment, statistical techniques (graphing, correlation, regression and others) are used to study the possible relationship between the two variables.

In modern data science the key goal is automation. Data science (like Artificial Intelligence field earlier) aims to automate decision-making, prediction, and production of knowledge. Based on the available information about the customer, shall a bank make a loan to this customer? Does a photograph contain a face? Does this face match an existing face in a database? Based on the phrase a search engine user typed, what web pages are most relevant to this phrase? In principle, each of these questions would be best answered if a human or a team spent sufficient time studying all relevant information and coming up with the answer. But this would require lots and lots of time for a single answer. Given the scale of information available in many situations (for example, the web contains approximately 14-15 billion web page), this time will approach infinity. Also, how many different conditions (variables) the data may contain, even infinite time will not help humans fully understand their effects.

Therefore, credit ranking systems, face recognition systems, search engines and countless other technological systems in our societies use data science algorithms and technologies to automate such tasks. In summary, the goal of data science is automation of human cognitive functions – trying to get computers to do cognitive tasks of humans, but much faster.

Achieving this goal is not easy because of what computer sciences call "semantic gap." This is the gap between knowledge that a human being can extract from some data, and how computer sees the same data. For example, looking at a photograph of a person, we can immediately detect that the photo shows a human figure, separate the figure from the background, understand what a person is wearing, face expression, and so on. But for a computer, a photograph is only a matrix of color pixels, each pixel defined by three numbers (contributions of red, green and blue making its color). A computer has to use this "low-level" information to try to guess what the image represents and how it represents it. Understanding a meaning of a text is another example of the semantic gap. A human reader understands what the text is about, but a computer can only "see" a set of letters separated by spaces.

Trying to "close the semantic gap" (this is the standard phrase in computer science publications) is one of the motivations for using multiple features. For example, the case of image analysis, a computer algorithm may extract various features from images, in addition to just the row RGB values of the pixels. Computer can identify regions that have similar color value and measure orientations of lines and properties of texture in many parts of an image. The hope is that together all these features will contain enough information for an algorithm to identify what an image represents.

In summary, 20th century statistical analysis and contemporary data science use variables in exactly the opposite way. Statistics and quantitative social science that uses it ideally wants to isolate one independent and one dependent variable, because the goal is understanding the phenomenon. Data science wants to use many features in the hope that together they contain the right information for automating recognition, classification, or another cognitive task.

Feature Space

Before we move on, a quick summary of what we learned so far about representing phenomena as data. We represent a phenomenon as a set of objects (also called data points, measurements, samples, or records) that have features (also called attributes, characteristics, variables, or metadata). Together, the objects and their features is what we mean by "data" (or "datasets"). Features can be represented in a variety of ways: whole and fractional numbers, categories, spatial coordinates, shapes and trajectories, dates, times, etc.

These are the basic requirements/conventions of modern data analysis and also data visualization. Now, let's start our next "lesson." To the concepts above (objects and features) we are going to add the third core concept: feature space.

We assume that our data is stored in a table. But now we will conceptualize our data table as a geometric space of many dimensions. Each feature becomes one of the dimensions. Each object becomes a point in this space. This is a "feature space," and it is the single most important and also most relevant for us in humanities the concept from contemporary data science, in my opinion.

The easiest way to understand this is by considering a familiar 2D scatter plot. Such a plot represents data in two dimensions. One dimension (X) corresponds to one feature (i.e., one column in a data table); the second dimension (Y) corresponds to a second feature (another column in the table). (Fig. 3 uses a space of two features to compare paintings Vincent van Gogh created in Paris and in Arles).

If we want to also add a third feature, we can make a three-dimensional scatterplot, if our software allows this. And if we have 10 features, our plot now conceptually exists in a 10-dimensional space. And so on. However, while mathematics and computer science have no problems working with spaces that may have arbitrary numbers of dimensions, we humans cannot see or plot them directly, because we exist physically and can only see in three dimensions. But we can still use computational techniques to think about objects in multi-dimensional spaces, and study their relations.

Use of Feature Space in Data Science

Once we represent some phenomenon or a process as a set of objects defined by many features, and conceptualize this representation as a multi-dimensional space, many analytical operations become possible. Many fundamental applications of data science correspond to such different operations, explicitly or implicitly.

For example, we can use a set of techniques called exploratory data analysis (described below) to "look" at the structure of the space and visualize it. To perform cluster analysis, we divide the space into parts, each containing points that are more similar to each other than to points outside this part. In classification, we identify the points belonging to two or more categories. ("Binary classification" deals with two categories; "multiclass classification" deals with more than two classes. If cluster analysis and classification sound similar, it is because they are, but while the first is completely automatic technique, classification needs some data that already has category information.) In many search algorithms, a computer finds the points in the space that are most similar to the input terms (these are points that are closest to the input in feature space – see the section on measuring distance in feature space below). Some of the recommendation algorithms work similarly – starting from the points that a user have previously favored, they find and display other points the closest to them (of course they do not show the points directly but the media objects represented by them such as movies, songs or people to follow on social media).

These operations rely on more basic ones such as computation of similarity/difference between points in a feature space. The degree or similarity/difference can be equated with the simple geometric distance between the points in the space).

I would like to mention a few more terms because they are so common in data science that you will inevitably encounter them. "Exploratory data analysis" is also called "unsupervised learning." In contrast, "supervised learning" needs part of the data already labeled as belonging to this or that category. Algorithms then use this labeled data along with its features to "learn" how to classify new data. The practical application of unsupervised learning is part of the field of "predictive analytics.")

Among the contemporary applications of data science, probably the most common is automatic classification. However, in my view it is the least interesting one for humanities. Why should we use computers to classify cultural artifacts, phenomena or activities into a small number of categories? Why not instead use computational methods to question the categories we already have, generate new ones, or create new cultural maps that relate cultural artifacts in original ways?

This is why this article does not go into any detail about the widely used data science methods you will find extensively covered in standard data sciences textbooks and courses – i.e., classification methods. But while these textbooks typically only devote a small part to exploratory data exploration, I think that for the humanities we need to reverse this ratio.

Figure 3: Comparing paintings created by van Gogh in Paris (left) and Arles (right) on brightness and saturation dimension. X-axis – average brightness; y-axis – average saturation. The visualization shows that on these dimensions, van Gogh's Paris paintings have more variability than his Arles paintings. We can also see that most paintings created in Arles occupy the same part of the brightness/saturation space as Paris paintings; only a small proportion of Arles's paintings explore the new part of this space (upper right corner). (Visualization by Lev Manovich / Software Studies Initiative).

Accordingly, in the rest of this article I will discuss data exploration techniques.

Difference as Distance in Feature Space

We learned that we could conceptualize a set of objects with many features as points in a multi-dimensional space. What are the benefits of such a representation for humanities?

The most basic method of humanities until now has been the same as in everyday human perception and cognition – comparison. (This is different from natural and social sciences that have been using mathematics, statistics, data visualization, computation and simulation to study their phenomena and objects.) In a 20th century art history class, a two-slide projector setup allowed for simultaneous viewing and comparison between two artifacts. Today in an art museum, a label next to one artifact point out the similarities between this artifact and a few other artifacts (or artists) in the same exhibition.

Manual comparison does not scale well for big data. For example, for our lab's project *On Broadway* that visualizes a single street in NYC using many data sources, we collected all publically visible Instagram images from the whole NYC area for five months in 2014. The result was 10.5 million images. Let's say we want to understand some patterns in this nice sample of contemporary vernacular photography – what are the subjects of these images, what are common and uncommon compositions, how this may differ between parts of NYC, how many

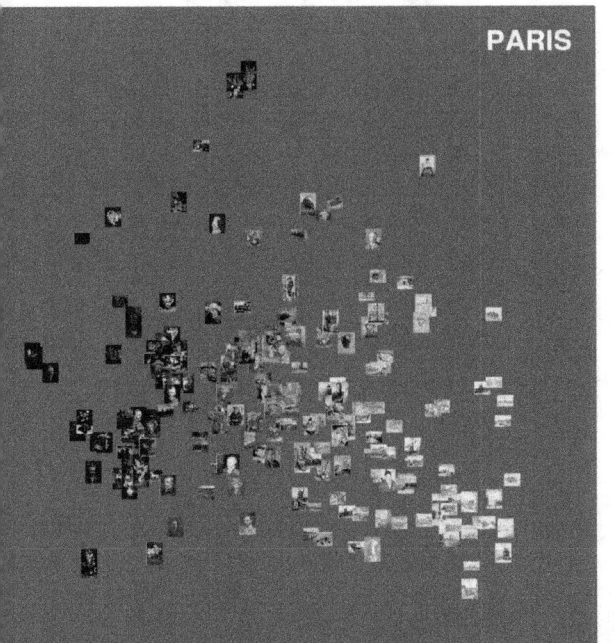
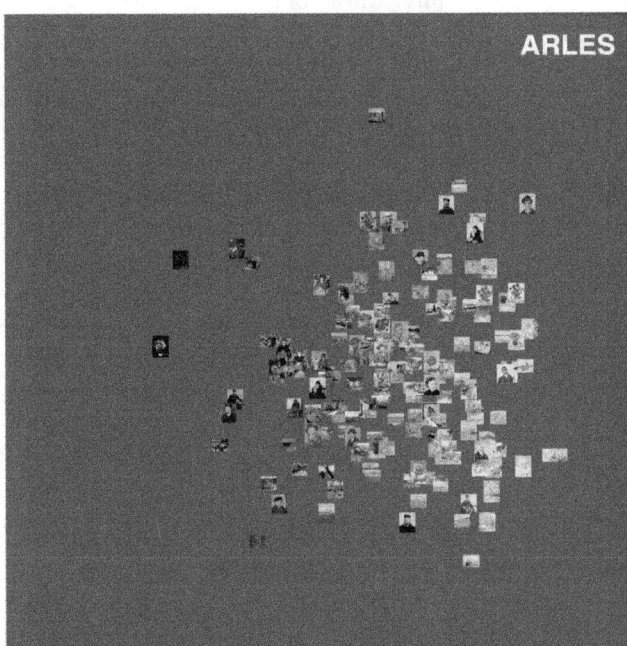

images are by people using techniques of professional commercial photography, and so on. Simply looking at all these images together will not allow us to answer such questions. And in fact, no popular commercial or free image management or sharing software or web service can even show that many images together in a single screen.

However, data science techniques can allow us to answer the questions such as the ones I posed above for very large datasets. By representing each image as a point in a space of many features, we can now compare them in quantitative way. In such representation, the visual difference between images is equated with a distance in feature space. This allows us to use computers to compute differences between as many images (or other types of cultural objects) as we want. Such computation then becomes basis for doing other more "high-level" operations: finding clusters of similar images; determining most popular and most unusual types of images; separating photos that use the language of professional photography, and so on.[10]

Using only two features is useful for developing an intuition about measuring distance in a multi-dimensional feature space. Consider a visualization in Fig. 3 showing images of van Gogh paintings that uses average brightness (X axis) and color saturation (Y axis). The geometric distance between any two images corresponds to the difference between them in brightness and saturation. Note that, of course, this example disregards all other types of difference: subject matter, composition, color palette, brushwork, and so. However, this is not only a limitation but also an advantage – by letting us isolate particular features, we can compare artifacts only on dimensions we want.

We can also compute and add as many features as we want. And although we may not be able to visualize and see directly the space of, for example, 50 or 500 features, we can still calculate the distance between points in this space. If the distance between two points is small, it means that the corresponding objects are similar to each other. If the distance between two points is large, it means that the corresponding objects are dissimilar to each other.

There are many ways to define and calculate distance, and data science uses a number of them. One popular way that is easiest to understand is using Euclidian geometry. (Another popular way is "cosine similarity," defined as the cosine of an angle between two vectors in feature space.) Note that in these calculations, we do not need to give equal weight to all features; if we believe that some of them are more important, we can also make them more important in the computation.

The concept of a geometric feature space allows us to take the most basic method of humanities – a comparison – and extend it to big cultural data. In the same time, it allows us (or forces us, if you prefer) to quantify the concept of difference. Rather than simply saying that artifact "A" is similar to artifact "B," and both "A" and "B" are dissimilar to "C," we can now express these relations in numbers. While this quantification may appear to be unnecessary if we are only considering a small number of artifacts, once we start dealing with thousands, tens of thousands, millions, and beyond, it becomes a very useful way of comparing them.

Exploring Feature Space

Let's say we want to understand some cultural field in a particular period – Ming Dynasty Chinese painting, realist art in Europe in late 19th century, graphic design in 1990s, social media photography in early 2010s, etc. What kinds of subject matter (if the field has a subject matter), styles and techniques are present? How they develop over time? Which of them were more popular and which were less popular? Art historians so far relied on human brain's abilities that developed evolutionary to see patterns and understand similarity and difference between sets of artifacts. They seemed to do well without using mathematics, graphic methods, statistics, computation, or contemporary data science. But the price for this "success" was the most extreme exclusion – considering only tiny sample of "important" or "best" works from every period or field. In the words of the pioneer of digital humanities Franko Moretti,

" What does it mean, studying world literature? How do we do it? I work on West European narrative between 1790 and 1930, and already feel like a charlatan outside of Britain or France... 'I work on West European narrative, etc....' Not really, I work on its canonical fraction, which is not even one per cent of published literature. And again, some people have read more, but the point is that there are thirty thousand nineteenth-century British novels out there, forty, fifty, sixty thousand—no one really knows, no one has read them, no one ever will. And then there are French novels, Chinese, Argentinian, American...[11] "

Moretti's point certainly applies to all other humanities fields; and it applies even more to the analysis of contemporary culture. Who can look at even a tiniest percentage of photos shared on Instagram every hour – or for example hundreds of million Instagram photos with a tag #fashion? Who can visit hundreds of cities around the world in a single month to understand the differences in street fashion between all of them? Who can browse through billions of web pages to understand the landscape of current web design?

Let's apply the concepts we learned – objects, features, feature space, distance in feature space, and various operations this representation allows (exploration, clustering, etc.) to this problem. First we need create an appropriate data set. As we already know, this means represent some cultural field as a large set of objects with various features. Each feature captures some characteristic of the objects. The features can use existing metadata (such as dates or names), extracted automatically by a computer, or added manually (in social sciences, this process is called "coding," in humanities, we call this "annotation" or "tagging").

The objects can be photographs, songs, novels, paintings, websites, user generated content on social networks, or any other large set of cultural artifacts selected using some criteria. They can be all works of a single creator, if we want to understand how her/his works are related to each other. Instead of the cultural artifacts, the objects in our representation can be also individual cultural consumers and features can represent some characteristics of their cultural activities: for example, web sites visited by a person, a trajectory though a museum and time spent looking at particular artworks, or the positions of faces in selfie photos (see our project http://www.selfiecity.net for the analysis of such data.)

Once we represent some cultural field or cultural activity field as data (objects and their features), we can conceptualize each object as a point in a multi-dimensional feature space. This allows us to use "exploratory data analysis" techniques from data science and also techniques from data visualization field to investigate the "shape" of this feature space.

The space may have different structures: all points may cluster together, or form a few clusters, or lie at approximately equal distances from each other, etc. Any of these patterns will have an appropriate cultural interpretation. If most points form a single cluster, this means that in a particular cultural field most works/activities have similar characteristics, and only a small number are significantly different. Or we can find a few large clusters that lie at sufficient distances from each other (this can be quantified by measuring distances between the centers of the clusters.). And if we find that there are no clusters, this means that a given cultural space has a high degree of variability, and every work is significantly different from the rest.[12]

Note that just as it was the case with van Gogh example, even if we use many different features, we cannot be sure that we have captured the right information to quantify difference as we humans see it. But producing a single "correct" map should not our main goal. Every selection of features and choice of parameters of the algorithm will create a different map of cultural artifacts we are interested in. And every map can show us something new.

Using modern data analysis and visualization software, we can generate multiple views of the same data quickly and compare them. This helps us to expand our understanding of a cultural phenomenon, and also notice the relations and patterns we did not see before. In other words, data science allows us not only just to see the data that is too big for our unaided perception and cognition; it also allows us to see data of any size (including very familiar canonical cultural datasets) *differently*.

Dimension Reduction

We want to explore the structure of a feature space: the presence, positions and the shapes of clusters, the distances between them, and the average distances between individual points. How to do this? It will be great if we can visualize this space. If we only have two features, we can directly map each of them into one dimension and create a conventional 2-D scatterplot. If we have many features, a space of many dimensions can be represented as a series of separate scatter plots, each plot showing a pair of features. This visualization technique is called a scatterplot matrix.

Scatterplot matrixes become less useful if we have lots of dimensions. Each plot only shows a particular projection of the space onto two dimensions, i.e., a single flat surface. If the shapes of point clusters are truly multi-dimensional,

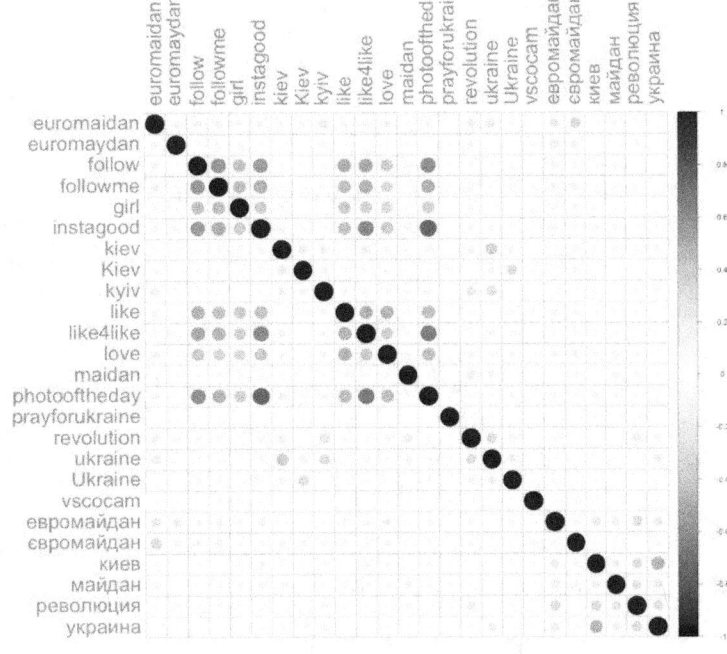

Figure 4: Heat map visualization of top tags assigned by Instagram users to images shared in the center of Kyiv during February 2014 Maidan revolution in Ukraine. Using Instagram API, we collected images for February 17-22. During this period 6,165 Instagram users shared 13,208 images which they tagged with the total of 21,465 tags (5845 unique tags). Visualization shows 25 most frequently used tags. The intensity of color/size indicates how frequently the two tags were used together. (Visualization by Lev Manovich / Software Studies Initiative.)

studying a large number of separate 2-D plots may not help us to see these shapes.

Another method for visualizing points in a space of many dimensions (i.e., many features) is to use a distance matrix. Distance matrix is computed directly from a data table. In a distance matrix, each cell represents a numerical distance between two objects from the original table. By converting the values of the cells into gray tones, colors, or shapes, we can turn the distance matrix into a visualization. Such visualization is called a heat map. Like scatterplot matrixes, heat maps can also quickly become very dense as we add features, and they also have the same limitation of making it hard to see the shapes of multi-dimensional clusters. Fig. 4 is an example of a heatmap visualizations used to explore tags assigned by Instagram users to images they share.

Data science developed another approach for seeing and interpreting the structure of a space of many dimensions. It is called dimension reduction. Along with objects, features, feature space and distances, dimension reduction is another fundamental concept of data science important for humanities.

Dimension reduction is the most widely used approach today for exploring data that has arbitrary larger number of features. It refers to various algorithms that create a low dimension representation of a multi-dimensional space. If this new representation only has two or three dimensions, we can visualize it using one or two standard 2D scatterplots.

Note that typically each axis in such scatterplot(s) no longer corresponds to a single feature. Instead, it represents a combination of various features. This is the serious challenge of dimension reduction algorithms – while they allow us to represent data using scatterplots where we can see the structure of a space easily, it can be quite challenging to interpret the meaning of each dimension. But even if we cannot say exactly what each axis represents, we can still study the shape of the space, the presence or absence of clusters, and the relative distances between points.

Dimension reduction is a projection of a space of many dimensions into a fewer dimensions – in the same way as a shadow of a person is a projection of a body in three dimensions into two dimensions. Depending on the position of the sun, some shadows will be more informative than others. (For example, if the sun is directly above my head, my shadow becomes very short, and my body shape is represented in a very distorted way. But if the sun is at 30 or 45 degree angle, my shadow will contain more information.) Similarly, the idea of dimension reduction is to preserve as much of the original information as possible. But it is crucial to keep in mind that some information will be always lost.

Different dimension reduction techniques use different criteria as to what kind of information should be preserved and how this is to be achieved. The following are among three very widely used data exploration methods that use dimension reduction:

Multi-dimensional scaling (MDS): We want to preserve the relative distances between points in a multi-dimensional space while projecting it into a lower dimension space.

Principal Component Analysis (PCA): We want to preserve most variability (spread of the data) when we go from all to fewer dimensions.

Factor analysis: Similar to MDS and PCA, but its original motivation was different. The idea of factor analysis is to extract "factors" – a smaller number of "hidden" variables that are responsible for the larger set of observed (recorded, measured) variables.[13]

Fig. 5 is an example of MDS visualization. We explore top 25 Instagram's tags for 13,208 images of Kyiv during February 2014 Maidan revolution in Ukraine, and find distinct semantic clusters.

Figure 5: Visualization of the data from Fig. 4 using multi-dimensional scaling (MDS). The tags that are often used together appear close to each other in the plot. On the right, we see a tight cluster of the tags that represent the "universal" Instagram language: #like, #follow, #instagood, etc. (these same tags are popular in lots of locations around the world). On the left, we see another cluster of tags associated with Maidan revolution. The visualization suggests that there is little interaction between these two types of tags: one group of Instagram users was using generic tags while another group was primarily tagging the local and specific events.

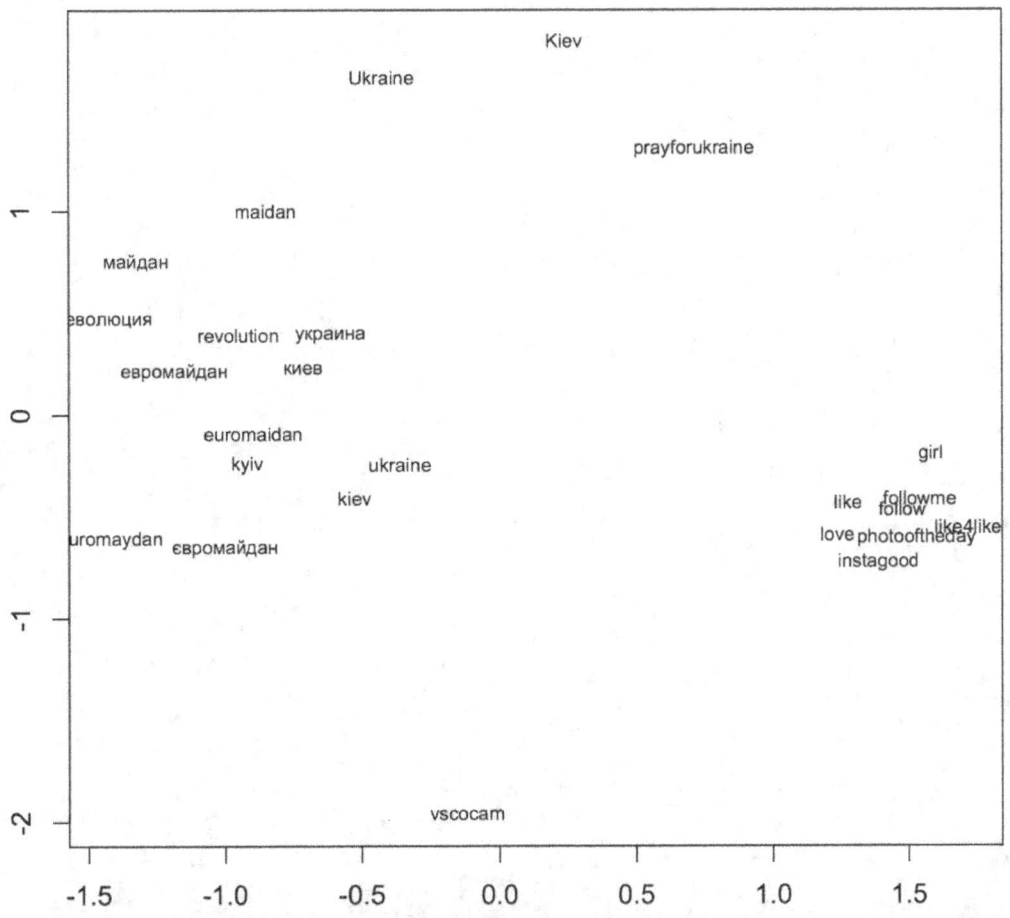

Fig. 6 shows an example of a visualization of approximately 6000 paintings of French Impressionists that uses PCA. In such visualization, images that are similar to each in terms of particular visual features are grouped together. Such visualizations allow us to compare many images to each other, and understand patterns of similarity and difference in large visual datasets.

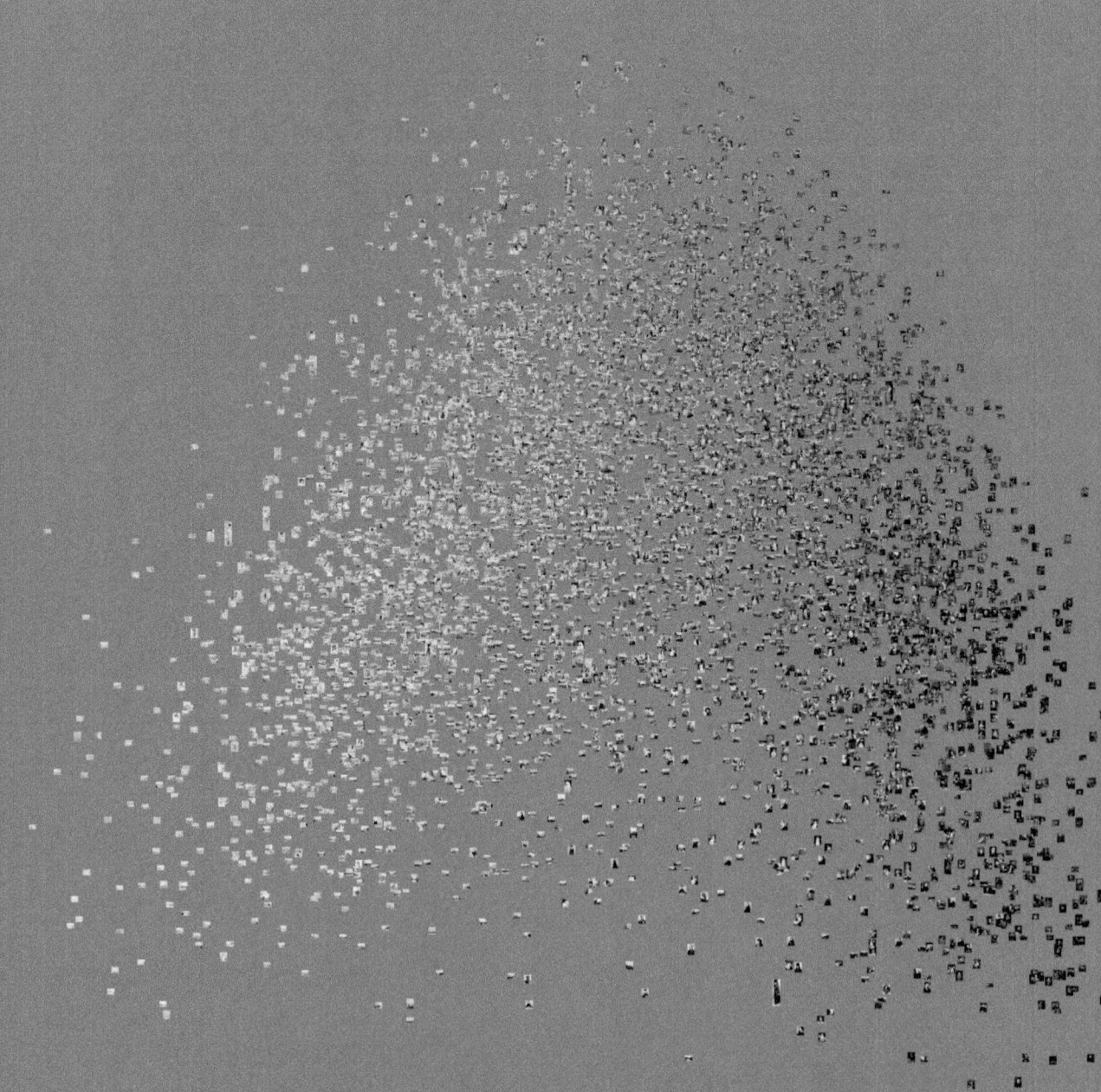

Conclusion

To explore is to compare. And to compare, we need first to see. To see big cultural data, we need to turn to data science.

Until the 21st century, we typically compared small numbers of artifacts, and the use of our human cognitive capacities unaided by machines was considered to be sufficient. But today, if we want to compare tens of thousands or millions of cultural artifacts (born digital user generated content is a prime example of such scales, but some digitized collections of historical artifacts can be also quite large) we have no choice but to use computational methods. In other words: To "see" contemporary culture requires use of computers and data science.

This computer "vision" can be understood as extension of the most basic act (or method) of humanities – comparing cultural artifacts (or periods, authors, genres, movements, themes, techniques, topics, etc.) So while computer-enabled seeing enabled by data science may be radical in terms of its scale – how much you can see in one "glance," so to speak – it continues the humanities' traditional methodology.

In this article I introduced a number of core concepts of data science: *objects, features, feature space, measuring distance in feature space, dimension reduction.* In my view, they are most basic and fundamental concepts of the field *relevant to humanities*. They enable exploration of large data, but they are also behind other areas of data science and their industry applications. In fact, they are as central to our "big data society" as other main cultural techniques we use to represent and reason about the world and each other – natural languages, lens-based photo and video imaging, material technologies for preserving and accessing information (paper, printing, digital media, etc.), counting, or calculus. They form data society's "mind" – the particular ways of encountering, understanding, and acting on the world and the humans specific to our time.

Figure 6: Example of a visualization of an image collection using Principal Component Analysis. The data set is digital images of approximately 6000 paintings by French Impressionists. We extracted 200 separate features from each image, describing its color characteristics, contrast, shapes, textures and some aspects of composition. We then used Principal Component Analysis to reduce the space of 200 features to a smaller number of dimensions, and visualized the first two dimensions. In a visualization, images that are similar to each in terms of features we extracted are grouped together. One interesting finding is that the types of images popularly associated with Impressionism (lower left part) constitute only a smaller part of the larger set of artworks created by these artists. At least half of the images turn to be rather traditional and more typical of classical 19th century painting (darker tones and warm colors.) Note that our data set contain only approximately ½ of all painting and pastels created by participants in Impressionist exhibitions in 1874-1886. (Visualization by Lev Manovich / Software Studies Initiative).

Notes

[1] Acknowledgments: This article draws on the research by Software Studies Initiative between 2007 and 2015. I would like to thank all graduate and undergraduate students who participated in our projects and our external collaborators. Our work was supported by The Andrew Mellon

Foundation, The National Endowment for the Humanities, The National Science Foundation, National Energy Research Scientific Computing Center (NERSC), The Graduate Center, City University of New York (CUNY), California Institute for Telecommunications and Information Technology (Calit2), University of California Humanities Research Institute, Singapore Ministry of Education, Museum of Modern Art (NYC) and New York Public Library.

2 Adrian Raftery, "Statistics in Sociology, 1950-2000: A Selective Review." Sociological Methodology 31 (2001): 1-45, https://www.stat.washington.edu/raftery/Research/PDF/socmeth2001.pdf (accessed April 24, 2015).

[3] For example, David Hand, Heikki Mannila, and Padhraic Smyth, *Principles of Data Mining* (Cambridge, Mass.: The MIT Press, 2001); Jure Leskovec, Anand Rajaraman, and Jeff Ullman, *Mining of Massive Datasets*. 2n edition (Cambridge: Cambridge University Press, 2014); Nina Zumel and John Mount, *Practical Data Science with R* (Shelter Island: Manning Publications, 2014).

[4] MoMA (Museum of Modern Art), Network diagram of the artists in *Inventing Abstraction, 1910-1925* exhibition (2012), http://www.moma.org/interactives/exhibitions/2012/inventingabstraction/?page=connections (accessed April 24, 2015).

[5] For historical examples, see Michael Friendly and Daniel Denis, "Milestones in the History of Thematic Cartography, Statistical Graphics, and Data Visualization" (n.d.), http://datavis.ca/milestones/ (accessed April 24, 2015).

[6] Michael Friendly and Daniel Denis, "The Early Origins and Development of the Scatterplot," *Journal of the History of the Behavioral Sciences* 41, no. 2 (2005): 103–130, http://www.datavis.ca/papers/friendly-scat.pdf (accessed April 24, 2015).

[7] Quoted in Garabed Eknoyan, "Adolphe Quetelet (1796–1874)—the average man and indices of obesity," *Nephrology Dialysis Transplantation* 23, no. 1 (2008): 47-51, http://ndt.oxfordjournals.org/content/23/1/47.full (accessed April 24, 2015).

[8] Émile Durkheim, *Le Suicide. Étude de Sociologie* (Paris, 1897).

[9] For a highly influential presentation of statistics in this period, see Ronald A. Fisher, *Statistical Methods for Research Workers* (Edinburgh: Oliver and Boyd, 1925), http://psychclassics.yorku.ca/Fisher/Methods/index.htm (accessed April 24, 2015).

[10] For one of the first publications in now what is a big field of computational analysis of large photo datasets, see Ritendra Datta et al., "Studying aesthetics in photographic images using a computational approach," *ECCV'06 Proceedings of the 9th European conference on Computer Vision* Volume Part III (2006): 288-301.

[11] Franko Moretti, "Conjectures on World Literature," *New Left Review* 1, January-February (2000): 55, http://newleftreview.org/II/1/franco-moretti-conjectures-on-world-literature (accessed April 24, 2015).

[12] See Lev Manovich, "Mondrian vs Rothko: footprints and evolution in style space," 2011, http://lab.softwarestudies.com/2011/06/mondrian-vs-rothko-footprints-and.html (accessed April 24, 2015).

[13] For one of the original formulation of factor analysis in psychology, see Louis Leon Thurstone, "Vectors of Mind," *Psychological Review* 41 (1934): 1-32, http://psychclassics.yorku.ca/Thurstone/ (accessed April 24, 2015).

Bibliography

Datta, Ritendra, Dhiraj Joshi, Jia Li, and James Wang. "Studying aesthetics in photographic images using a computational approach." *ECCV'06 Proceedings of the 9th European conference on Computer Vision* Volume Part III (2006): 288-301.

Durkheim, Émile. *Le Suicide. Étude de Sociologie*. Paris, 1897.

Fisher, Ronald A. *Statistical Methods for Research Workers*. Edinburgh: Oliver and Boyd, 1925. http://psychclassics.yorku.ca/Fisher/Methods/index.htm

Friendly, Michael and Daniel Denis. "The Early Origins and Development of the Scatterplot." *Journal of the History of the Behavioral Sciences* 41, no. 2 (2005): 103-130. http://www.datavis.ca/papers/friendly-scat.pdf

---. "Milestones in the History of Thematic Cartography, Statistical Graphics, and Data Visualization." N.d. http://datavis.ca/milestones/

Eknoyan, Garabed. "Adolphe Quetelet (1796-1874)—the average man and indices of obesity." *Nephrology Dialysis Transplantation* 23, no. 1 (2008): 47-51. http://ndt.oxfordjournals.org/content/23/1/47.full

Hand, David, Heikki Mannila, and Padhraic Smyth. *Principles of Data Mining*. Cambridge, Mass.: The MIT Press, 2001.

Leskovec, Jure, Anand Rajaraman, and Jeff Ullman. *Mining of Massive Datasets*. 2n edition. Cambridge: Cambridge University Press, 2014. Full book text is available at http://www.mmds.org/.

Manovich, Lev. "Mondrian vs Rothko: footprints and evolution in style space." 2011. http://lab.softwarestudies.com/2011/06/mondrian-vs-rothko-footprints-and.html

MoMA (Museum of Modern Art). Network diagram of the artists in *Inventing Abstraction, 1910-1925* exhibition. 2012. http://www.moma.org/interactives/exhibitions/2012/inventingabstraction/?page=connections

Moretti, Franko. "Conjectures on World Literature." *New Left Review* 1, January-February (2000): 54-68. http://newleftreview.org/II/1/franco-moretti-conjectures-on-world-literature

Raftery, Adrian. "Statistics in Sociology, 1950-2000: A Selective Review." *Sociological Methodology* 31 (2001): 1-45. https://www.stat.washington.edu/raftery/Research/PDF/socmeth2001.pdf

Thurstone, Louis Leon. "Vectors of Mind." *Psychological Review* 41 (1934): 1-32. (Address of the president before the American Psychological Association, Chicago meeting, September, 1933.) http://psychclassics.yorku.ca/Thurstone/

Zumel, Nina and John Mount. *Practical Data Science with R*. Shelter Island: Manning Publications, 2014.

Lev Manovich is a Professor of Computer Science at The Graduate Center, City University of New York, and founder and director of Software Studies Initiative.

He is the author of seven books including Software Takes Command (Bloomsbury Academic, 2013), Soft Cinema: Navigating the Database (The MIT Press, 2005), and The Language of New Media (The MIT Press, 2001) which was described as "the most suggestive and broad ranging media history since Marshall McLuhan." In 2014 he was included in the list of 50 "most interesting people building the future" (The Verge).

Correspondence e-mail: manovich.lev@gmail.com

What is Digital Art History?

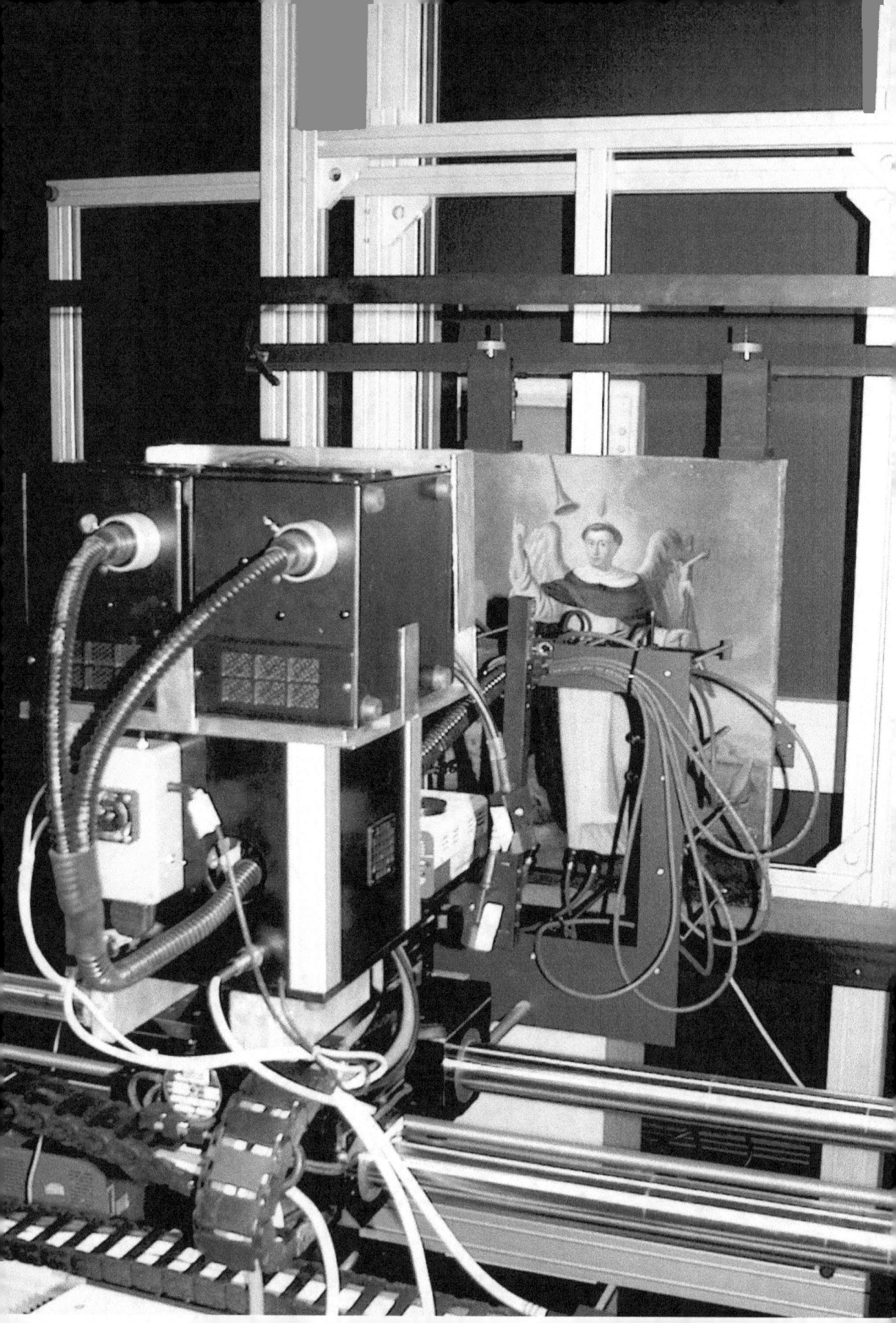

Peer-Reviewed

Forgotten Genealogies: Brief Reflections on the History of Digital Art History

Benjamin Zweig

Abstract: The past five years have witnessed a growing interest amongst art historians in the potential of digital projects to impact, if not transform, the discipline. A steep rise in conferences and institutes dedicated to digital art history, along with funding opportunities and institutional support, has accelerated the rate at which art historians are now engaging with digital techniques. With this new visibility, art historians have criticized themselves for lagging behind other disciplines such as history and archaeology. This article questions the assumption that art historians have been slow to embrace digital tools and methods through a brief historical examination of projects undertaken by institutions and scholars during the infancy of art history computing: the early 1980s through the early 1990s. Using Johanna Drucker's distinction of the "digitized" and "digital" iterations of art history, this essay traces the genealogies of both categories, arguing that scholars have been more active in theorizing, practicing and creating digital methods than is often seen to be the case. Ultimately, this essay is an attempt to help define from a historical perspective what "digital art history" is and how it has been practiced.

Keywords: historiography, databases, art history, methodology, museum, digital, digitized

Introduction[1]

In her 2012 report for the Kress Foundation *Transitioning to a Digital World: Art History, Its Research Centers, and Digital Scholarship*, Diane Zorich summarizes both the consternation that art historians have been left behind by the digital turn in the humanities and the skepticism that it is going to change the practices of the discipline in any meaningful way.[2] In her estimation, "There is a pervasive sense that the discipline is too cautious, moves too slowly, and has to "catch up" in the digital arena."[3] This perception is not a new one. In his 1992 article "Computer Applications in the History of Art," Anthony Hamber argues how "information

Figure 1: The VASARI Scanner. Date unknown.
(Photo: Kirk Martinez. Reproduced with permission)

technology within the world of the history of art has, until recently, lagged somewhat behind [other disciplines]."[4] Such attitudes have continued to circulate throughout art history. In the 2004 book *A Companion to Digital Humanities*, Michael Greenhalgh, a longtime supporter of art history computing, laments how it is "the human element [rather than the technological] that restricts obvious developments in the discipline."[5] The announcement for a conference on "Digital Art History" held at the Institute of Fine Arts, New York University, at the end of 2012 proclaims, "In the context of art history the integration of digital tools and processes has lagged, in varying degrees, in comparison to other disciplines like archaeology and literary studies."[6] And in a paper delivered at the conference "The Digital World of Art History 2013: From Theory to Practice" at the Index of Christian Art, Zorich argues that art history has been "slow at adopting the computational methodologies and analytic techniques that are enabled by new technologies," singling out as examples visualization, network analysis, and topic modeling.[7]

Rather than embracing the methodological innovations or challenges presented by computational practices, the argument goes, art historians have simply lapsed into using technology as ever-expanding slide libraries. Johanna Drucker makes this point in a 2013 article in the journal *Visual Resources*, in which she distinguishes between art historians who practice *digitized art history* and those who practice *digital art history*. According to Drucker, "[a] clear distinction has to be made between the use of online repositories and images, which is *digit-*

ized [emphasis in original] art history, and the use of analytic techniques enabled by computational technology that is the proper domain of *digital* [emphasis in original] art history."[8] In Drucker's view, the "digitized" iteration of art history propels traditional practices, exemplified by the online publication of image collections and born-digital periodicals such as *Nineteenth-Century Art Worldwide*. This iteration gives scholars quicker access to more materials without challenging the practices under which they work.[9] In contrast, the "digital" is "the use of analytic techniques enabled by computational technology," including structured metadata, network analysis, discourse analysis, virtual modeling, simulation, and the aggregation of materials from disparate geographic locations.[10]

With the steep rise of scholarly interest in using, theorizing, and funding the creation of digital tools and methodologies, it seems as though art historians are indeed playing catch-up. But art historians' engagement with both the *digitized* and the *digital* versions of art historical practice, as per Drucker, is more historically complex than current debates suggest. For instance, as early as 1981 the Getty Art History Information Program (AHIP), an antecedent of the Getty Research Institute, set out to facilitate the creation of sets of linked "data banks" by the Getty and a group of international partner institutions that included the National Gallery of Art, Washington, and the Witt Library.[11] In 1985, the group Computers and the History of Art (CHArt) was founded in London in order to bring together academics, museum professionals, and information technology specialists who were interested in pursuing computational practices, such as database creation and quantitative analysis, as well as developing new software and hardware with which to examine works of art.[12] CHArt began publishing a newsletter in 1986, a book in 1989, and an eponymous journal in 1990.[13] Indeed, 1990 also witnessed the first "Electronic Visualization and the Arts" (EVA) conference at the Imperial College, London. In 1997, Hubertus Kohle published the volume *Kunstgeschichte digital: eine Einführung für Praktiker und Studierende*, a collection of 15 essays exploring a diverse array of projects and theoretical positions on the relationship between art history and computers.[14] That same year, two unrelated articles were published exploring the intersection of art history and emerging technologies: "Digital Art History: A New Field for Collaboration" by Sally Promey and Miriam Stewart in *American Art*, and "Digital Culture and the Practices of Art and Art History" by Kathleen Cohen *et al* in *The Art Bulletin*.[15] And in 2005, CHArt published the volume *Digital Art History: A Subject in Transition*.[16]

In this short essay, I want to question the assumption that art history has lagged behind other humanities disciplines in its engagement with digital tools and techniques.[17] I approach the ontology of "digital art history" from a historical perspective rather than a technical or methodological one.[18] I want to sketch out the genealogies of "digital art history" itself to better understand how the practices and debates subsumed under this concept have taken shape. I do not attempt to tell the complete story. Indeed, I limit my chronological scope from roughly the early 1980s through the mid 1990s, and have selected just a few examples from a rich body of material. Ultimately, this essay is an attempt to help define from a historical perspective what "digital art history" is and how it has been practiced.

A Genealogy of "Digitized" Art History

Drucker's distinction between *digitized* and *digital* art history, while imperfect categories, affords us with a good point of entry from which to understand the history of doing art history digitally. Let us begin with the *digitized*, the creation of electronic databases and the digitization of works of art and image collections.

The earliest projects integrating computers with art history primarily emerged from museums and libraries in the late 1970s and the early 1980s.[19] As computers enabled cultural organizations to organize better large and sometimes poorly documented collections, museums and libraries from the United States and Europe saw the potential for collaboration and the cross-referencing of their collections. But there were complications. While computers allowed for the unprecedented exchange of information, disparate standards of cataloging practices made communication difficult. Several ambitious initiatives and groups sought to tackle this problem. For instance, in 1983 the international Architectural

Drawings Advisory Group (ADAG) first convened at the Center for Advanced Study in the Visual Arts (CASVA) in Washington in order to systematize cataloging standards that would ensure for scholars "a consistent set of research information across repositories, perhaps eventually, *through an electronic network* [emphasis added]."[20]

In 1986, a sub-group of four ADAG repositories and the Getty Trust, the Foundation for Documents of Architecture (FDA), was created for the purpose of addressing disparate cataloging practices for closely related drawings. In 1988-1989, and housed at the National Gallery in Washington, the FDA project staff was tasked with experimenting on a new cataloging system devised by AHIP that "would allow scholars to manipulate catalogue information in ways that would yield *new views of the material itself* [emphasis added]."[21] The ideal goal was not simply to reconcile cataloging practices through computers, but to use them as a means to find new research questions. They sought "to define what an electronic research environment might be."[22] While the FDA eventually concluded that the development of a computer network was beyond its reach, the ambition to develop such a project, and the foresight regarding its possibilities, was at the cutting edge of conceptualizing the intersection of art history with information technology.

Smaller institutions began independently testing the ideas floated by the ADAG and AHIP from an early date. In 1989, Janet Barnes, Keeper of the Ruskin Gallery, Sheffield, England, considered implementing a database that would function as both the first accurate catalog of the gallery's collection *and* as a multifaceted image retrieval system for users rather than a standard commercial inventory system.[23] The logic behind creating such a system was to follow the intentions of the art critic John Ruskin, who compiled the museum's collection, so that visitors could easily make connections between ostensibly unrelated artworks – effectively an early user-oriented and visually-constructed relational database. The ultimate fate of the project is sadly unclear.

1989 also witnessed the initiation of the ambitious and well-documented image-oriented database VASARI project, both a reference to Giorgio Vasari and an acronym for Visual Arts System for Archiving and Retrieval of Images.[24] VASARI was an international collaborative, bringing together scientific departments from the National Gallery, London, the Doerner Institute of the Bavarian State Galleries, Telecom Paris, the Louvre, and the Department of the History of Art, Birkbeck College, University of London, which handled much of the art historical and computer science aspects of the project.[25] The goal of VASARI was to create digital images of sufficiently high resolution that could replace photographs as the preferred recording system for artworks. VASARI did not rely on scanning existing images or transparencies into a database. Rather, it sought to create new colorimetric images taken directly from paintings, which involved the creation of a new type of scanner that recorded paintings frame by frame (or pixel by pixel) through seven simultaneous color filters, and then "mosaiced" them together using custom software (Fig. 1).[26] These images were to be far more accurate in terms of their color reproduction and color monitoring than analog photography.[27] Most interestingly, the VASARI project was envisioned as "machine independent," able to be transported from computer to computer and, ideally, over a network, rather than tied to a single workstation.[28] In this way, VASARI was conceived as a web-based project before the "web" was in the public consciousness – indeed, conceived of at the same moment as Tim Berners-Lee's revolutionary work at CERN.

In 1994, AHIP published *Humanities and Arts on the Information Highways*, one of the earliest "state of the field" reports for what would become better known as the "digital humanities."[29] The report extolled the possibilities presented by the exchange of information electronically, while also highlighting its many challenges, such as technological barriers, political apathy, and the undercapitalization of projects. The report lists many art history projects in their survey of important computer-based projects in the humanities and the arts (a number of which still function), including the MIT Museum Architecture Project, the Bibliography of the History of Art, the Save Outdoor Sculpture Project, the Witt Computer Index of Print Works, and the Census of Antique Art and Architecture Known to the Renaissance.[30]

The above projects are electronic databases or iterations of mostly pre-electronic initiatives. But the report goes deeper than summarizing then-current electronic projects. It enumerates a series of recommendations for the practice of creating and maintaining digital projects, such as enabling the "highest fidelity of representation of originals" and preserving object integrity through "technical methods such as color matching and compensation."[31] Moreover, the report encourages the development of new tools for humanities and arts computing, including building authoring tools that "exploit networked resources," "capture text, image, and sound in its editing and mark-up while capturing the history of different versions," "annotate videoclips, images, oral interviews, music, dance, and other cultural heritage information," and "support annotation systems that allow not only for personal commentary, but also for additions to the cumulative scholarly record."[32] AHIP was highly conscious of the impact that the digitization of source material could have on scholarly exchange while being equally aware of how electronic formats presented a host of particular challenges and possibilities.

There are many other notable examples of art historical projects that began testing the limits of technology's impact on image databasing in the 1980s and 1990s, such as the Visual Arts Network for the Exchange of Cultural Knowledge (VAN EYCK) project, a European international collaborative that sought to exchange text and image information between different art historical databases that could be searched simultaneously from remote terminals – a precursor of aggregator sites like Europeana or the Getty Research Portal.[33] The point to be taken from the above survey is that art historians have not simply been interested in creating a better slide library. For many years scholars have recognized the potential that the *digitized* iteration of art history held for organizing and working with both the objects of study and for scholarly collaboration; something that is becoming increasingly important with the move towards linked open data and the semantic web.

A Genealogy of "Digital" Art History

What, then, about the *digital* iteration of art historical practice that art historians are criticized for not practicing? Can this charge hold up to a scrutiny of the historical record?

Let us begin answering this question by examining one the earliest projects that sought to use computational techniques for art historical research: the pioneering MORELLI project, named after the physician and connoisseur Giovanni Morelli and initiated in the mid 1980s by William Vaughan, Professor of Art History at Birkbeck College. In short, MORELLI was a pattern recognition tool that automatically classified and analyzed the formal qualities of pictures.[34] Vaughan conceptualized the project as "a simple matching process...the visual equivalent of the 'word search' [feature]..."[35] But MORELLI did not rely on metadata as its organizing principle, as would be the case with a traditional database. Instead, features such as compositional configuration and tonality were to be derived directly from the process of digitization, which would then be compared across a base data set of 10,000 images.[36] Moreover, it used a monochrome low-resolution digital image of 64KB rather than large files, and was able to recognize within "reasonable limits" different copies of the same picture and differentiate formally similar pictures without confusion.[37]

According to Vaughan, the ultimate ambition of the project was to enable a *new* methodology in order "to make such visual sorting and selecting.... something that could genuinely be the basis of structured pictorial analysis."[38] Because the system relied on visual matching and sorting, in a fully implemented system the user could sift through an enormous visual archive, one beyond the capacity of human memorization, to find patterns and anomalies in the historical record; that is, to find if a particular type of composition is unique to one artist or one period, and, most importantly, to "link images together that cannot be found by means of textual reference."[39] MORELLI was thus envisioned as enabling a "visual syntax of forms" from which complex visual arguments could be made, and stands as an unheralded antecedent to contemporary projects like Image Plot.[40]

Vaughan's MORELLI project had a cognate in IBM Almaden's Query by Image and Video Content System (QBIC).[41] Like MORELLI, QBIC retrieved data from images not based on subject matter, as art historians might understand "content" to mean, but on the visual qualities of the image – line, color, patterns, textures, and shapes.[42] In theory, the system allowed a user to conduct queries such as "Find images with a red, round object,"

"Find images that have approximately 30-percent red and 15-percent blue colors," or "Find images that have 30 percent red and contain a blue textured object."[43] In 1993, the Department of Art and Art History at the University of California, Davis, put these ideas into practice and launched a pilot database using QBIC as a means of enabling better searching through the department's collection of 200,000 slides.[44] After the completion of initial testing using a data set of 2,000 images, the department concluded that QBIC's chief strength resided in its ability to *sort* artworks by aesthetic values rather than search for them. The value of applying the QBIC system to an image collection was to allow a user to sift quickly through large datasets to find hidden trends, relationships, or themes; the visual equivalent to computational methodologies such as text mining and topic modeling.

During the late 1980s and early 1990s, a number of art historians were also working on smaller-scale digital projects. For instance, around 1988, Marilyn Lavin began planning an interactive three-dimensional recreation of Piero della Francesca's *Legend of the True Cross* at Arezzo.[45] As she saw it, formats such as slides gave uniform scale to all images, unintentionally eliminating important aesthetic and experiential differences. The aim of the Piero project was to "present an electronic surrogate for the configuration of the fresco paintings as they appear to a visitor in the church," which would incorporate natural color, relative scale, and physical environment.[46] Lavin's project sought to use the digital environment to re-create one of the most persistent concerns of the history of art – understanding a work of art in its physical and historical context. The central problem tackled by Lavin's project was by no means a radical one; in fact, it was a rather conservative one. But the virtual modeling approach allowed for an "analytic flexibility" that still photography could not equal.[47]

One of the more interesting early digital projects (c. 1990) was Gilbert Herbert and Ita Heinze-Greenberg's statistical analysis of the profession of the architect in Palestine during the British Mandate of the 1920s and 1930s.[48] In contrast to the biographical approach (understandably) favored by most scholars, Herbert and Heinze-Greenberg organized a databank of 595 persons who had lived and worked in Palestine as architects between 1918 and 1948, of which 470 contained enough information to use in their study. The authors organized their data by the years of immigration of architects into Palestine, the countries from which they emigrated, the country of education of architects born in Palestine, and the country of education of architects who qualified for the profession after immigration. Some of the conclusions they reached by quantitative analysis included the large number of German-born and German-educated architects, many who studied at the Bauhaus; that while the number of British-born architects was small, a large group of Russian and Polish-born architects trained in the United Kingdom; and that during the first decade of the mandate, 85% of immigrant architects had been in the country less than ten years.[49]

The value of such quantitative studies as Herbert and Heinze-Greenberg's for art history is that they can problematize the weighty claims put forth by scholars based upon very small data sets. By displacing the centrality of exceptional works of art or individual biographies into larger networks, this approach can function as a research method that raises new questions about historical events and as a potential mode of historiographic critique. As the foundation for methods such as topic modeling and data mining, the quantitative analysis of art historical data can be both a challenge and a *complement* to the case-study model of practice.

Conclusion

This brief enumerative trip into the historical record shows how art historians have been engaged in theorizing and using computational technologies and techniques since the 1980s. As noted earlier, the projects outlined here merely scratch the surface of a much richer history. While working digitally has been a small subset of disciplinary practice, it has by no means been absent. Many of the challenges these early forays in the digital world faced and that sadly could not be addressed here – funding, sustainability, archiving, copyright, technological obsolescence, documentation, tenure consideration, peer evaluation – will remain issues that art historians must tackle as the field moves forward. By gazing at the recent past, the field can recognize these pioneering contributions and learn from their ambitions. Technology has reached a point where it is now easier (but by no means easy) to experiment with digital tools and methods, from using content management systems, to analyzing collection metadata released by museums, to employing open-source programs such as the visualization tool Gephi and the mapping program QGIS. But as digital art history continues to grow, as the problems it addresses become more sophisticated, as we work to define the tenets under which it functions, as it occupies a more central place in the discipline, and as scholars become more active in the creation of digital tools, we should be careful not to forget that the digital itself has formed part of the larger history of art history.

Notes

[1] For their most valuable input and support, I would like to thank Deans Elizabeth Cropper, Peter Lukehart, and Therese O'Malley at the Center For Advanced Study in the Visual Arts, Paul Jaskot, Susan Siegfried, Kirk Martinez, the journal's editors, and the two anonymous reviewers.

[2] Diane Zorich, *Transitioning to a Digital World: Art History, Its Research Centers, and Digital Scholarship* (New York: Samuel H. Kress Foundation, 2012), esp. 6, 14, 20. Available at: http://www.kressfoundation.org/uploadedFiles/Sponsored_Research/Research/Zorich_TransitioningDigitalWorld.pdf

[3] Ibid, 20.

[4] Anthony Hamber, "Computer Applications in the History of Art: A perspective from Birkbeck College, University of London," *Extrait de la Revue Informatique et Statistique dans les Sciences humaines*, Vol. 28, No. 1 (1992), 79-91.

[5] Michael Greenhalgh, "Art History," *A Companion to Digital Humanities* (Oxford: Blackwell, 2004), 41. Book available at: http://www.digitalhumanities.org/companion/

[6] http://www.nyu.edu/gsas/dept/fineart/research/mellon/mellon-digital.htm

[7] Diane Zorich, "The "Art" of Digital Art History," presented at the Index of Christian Art, Princeton University, June 26, 2013. Available at: http://ica.princeton.edu/digitalbooks/digitalworldofarthistory2013/7.D.Zorich.pdf

[8] Johanna Drucker, "Is There a "Digital" Art History?" *Visual Resources: An International Journal of Documentation*, Vol. 29, No. 1-2 (2013), 7.
[9] Ibid.
[10] Ibid.
[11] A brief overview available at: http://socialarchive.iath.virginia.edu/xtf/view?docId=getty-art-history-information-program-cr.xml
[12] For a brief discussion of the founding of CHArt, see Jean Miles, "Introduction," *Computers and the History of Art*, Vol. 1, No. 1 (1990), 1-2; also Hamber, "Computer Applications," 81.
[13] A full list of CHArt programs and publications available at: www.chart.ac.uk
[14] *Kunstgeschichte digital: eine Einführung für Praktiker und Studierende*, ed. Hubertus Kohle (Berlin: Dietrich Reimer Verlag, 1997).
[15] Sally M. Promey and Miriam Stewart, "Digital Art History: A New Field for Collaboration," *American Art*, Vol. 11, No. 2 (1997), 36-41; Kathleen Cohen, James Elkins, Marilyn Aronberg Lavin, Nancy Macko, Gary Schwartz, Susan L. Siegfried and Barbara Maria Stafford, "Digital Culture and the Practices of Art and Art History," *The Art Bulletin*, Vol. 79, No. 2 (1997), 187-216.
[16] *Digital Art History: A Subject in Transition*, ed. Anna Bentkowska-Kafel, Trish Cashen, and Hazel Gardiner (Bristol: Intellect Books, 2005).
[17] Elizabeth Cropper, Dean of the Center for Advanced Study in the Visual Arts (CASVA), made a similar point in her introductory remarks to the conference "New Projects in Digital Art History," held at the National Gallery of Art, Washington D.C., November 21, 2014.
[18] Indeed, the history of the digital humanities has received little attention. See Julianne Nyhan, Andrew Flinn, and Anne Welsh, "Oral History and the Hidden Histories project: towards histories of computing in the humanities," *Digital Scholarship in the Humanities*, Vol. 30, No. 1 (2015), 71-85. Thanks to Paul Jaskot for alerting me to this essay. Available at: http://dsh.oxfordjournals.org/content/30/1/71
[19] The history of museums and technology deserves a much fuller investigation than can be done here.
[20] Vicki Porter and Robin Thomas, *A Guide to the Description of Architectural Drawings* (New York: G.K. Hall & Co., 1994), xvii.
[21] Ibid, xix.
[22] Ibid.
[23] Janet Barnes and Alan Griffiths, "Creating an image database for the Collection of the Guild of St. George Ruskin Gallery, Sheffield, UK," *Computers and the History of Art*, Vol. 3, No. 1 (1992), 17-24.
[24] Anthony Hamber, "The VASARI Project," *Computers and the History of Art*, Vol. 1, No. 2 (1990), 3-19.
[25] For the entire list of partners, see Ibid, 3-4.
[26] Ibid.
[27] Ibid, 4-5.
[28] Ibid, 5.
[29] *Humanities and Arts on the Information Highways: A Profile. Final Report.* (Santa Monica: Getty Art History Information Program, 1994). Available at: http://www.cni.org/resources/historical-resources/humanities-and-art-on-the-information-highways
[30] Ibid, 43-44.
[31] Ibid, 31.
[32] Ibid, 32.
[33] Colum Hourihane and John Sunderland, "The Van Eyck Project, Information Exchange in Art Libraries," *Computers and the History of Art*, Vol. 5, No. 1 (1992), 25-40.
[34] William Vaughan, "The Automated Connoisseur: Image Analysis and Art History," *History and Computing*, ed. Peter Denley and Deian Hopkin (Manchester: Manchester University Press, 1987), 215-221; idem, "Automated Picture Referencing: A Further look at 'Morelli'," *Computers and the History of Art*, Vol. 2, No. 2 (1992), 7-18; idem, "Computergestützte Bildrecherche und Bildanalyse," *Kunstgeschichte digital*, 97-105.
[35] Vaughan, "Automated Picture Referencing," 9.
[36] Ibid, 15.
[37] Hamber, "Computer Applications," 82.
[38] Vaughan, "Automated Picture Referencing," 8-9.
[39] Ibid, 17.
[40] Image Plot: http://lab.softwarestudies.com/p/imageplot.html
[41] It is unclear to me when exactly IBM began developing QBIC. It was well underway by 1992-1993. See note 42.
[42] Myron Flickner, Harpeet Sawhney, Wayne Niblack, Jonathan Ashley, Qian Huang, Byron Dom, Monika Gorkani, Jim Hafner, Denis Lee, Dragutin Petkovic, David Steele, and Peter Yanker, "Query by Image and Video Content: The QBIC System," *IEEE Computer*, Vol. 28, No. 9 (1995), 23-32.
[43] Ibid. 25.
[44] Bonnie Holt, Ken Weiss, Wayne Niblack, Myron

Flickner, and Dragutin Petkovic, "The QBIC Project in the Department of Art and Art History at UC Davis," *Proceedings of the Annual ASIS Meeting*, Vol. 34 (1997), 189-195.

[45] Marilyn Aronberg Lavin, "Researching Visual Images with Computer Graphics," *Computers and the History of Art*, Vol. 2, No. 2 (1992), 1-5. The project, albeit in a very different form than the original, is available at: http://projects.ias.edu/pierotruecross/

[46] Ibid, 2.

[47] Drucker makes a good point of highlighting the "analytical flexibility" of virtual reconstructions. Drucker, "Is There a "Digital" Art History?" 11.

[48] Gilbert Herbert and Ita Heinze-Greenberg, "The Anatomy of a Profession: Architects in Palestine during the British Mandate," *Computers and the History of Art*, Vol. 4, No. 1 (1993), 75-85.

[49] Ibid, 80-84.

Bibliography

Barnes, Janet and Alan Griffiths. "Creating an image database for the Collection of the Guild of St. George Ruskin Gallery, Sheffield, UK." *Computers and the History of Art* 3, No. 1 (1992): 17-24.

Bentkowska-Kafel, Anna, Trish Cashen, and Hazel Gardiner, ed. *Digital Art History: A Subject in Transition*. Bristol: Intellect Books, 2005.

Cohen, Kathleen, James Elkins, Marilyn Aronberg Lavin, Nancy Macko, Gary Schwartz, Susan L. Siegfried and Barbara Maria Stafford. "Digital Culture and the Practices of Art and Art History." *The Art Bulletin* 79, No. 2 (1997): 187-216.

Drucker, Johanna. "Is there a Digital Art History?" *Visual Resources: An International Journal of Documentation* 29, No. 1 (2013): 5-13.

Flickner, Myron, Harpeet Sawhney, Wayne Niblack, Jonathan Ashley, Qian Huang, Byron Dom, Monika Gorkani, Jim Hafner, Denis Lee, Dragutin Petkovic, David Steele, and Peter Yanker. "Query by Image and Video Content: The QBIC System." *IEEE Computer* 28, No. 9 (1995): 23-32.

Greenhalgh, Michael. "Art History." In *A Companion to Digital Humanities*, edited by Susan Schreibman, Ray Siemens, and John Unsworth, 31-45. Oxford: Blackwell Publishing, 2004.

Hamber, Anthony. "The VASARI Project." *Computers and the History of Art* 1, No. 2 (1990): 3-19.

--- "Computer Applications in the History of Art: A perspective from Birkbeck College, University of London." *Extrait de la Revue Informatique et Statistique dans les Sciences humaines* 28, No. 1 (1992): 79-91.

Herbert, Gilbert and Ita Heinze-Greenberg. "The Anatomy of a Profession: Architects in Palestine during the British Mandate." *Computers and the History of Art* 4, No. 1 (1993): 75-85.

Holt, Bonnie, Ken Weiss, Wayne Niblack, Myron Flickner, and Dragutin Petkovic. "The QBIC Project in the Department of Art and Art History at UC Davis." *Proceedings of the Annual ASIS Meeting* 34 (1997): 189-195.

Hourihane, Colum, and John Sunderland. "The Van Eyck Project, Information Exchange in Art Libraries." *Computers and the History of Art* 5, No. 1 (1992): 25-40.

Humanities and Arts on the Information Highways: A Profile. Final Report. Santa Monica: Getty Art History Information Program, 1994.

Kohle, Hubertus, ed. *Kunstgeschichte digital: eine Einführung für Praktiker und Studierende*. Berlin: Dietrich Reimer Verlag, 1997.

Lavin, Marilyn Aronberg. "Researching Visual Images with Computer Graphics." *Computers and the History of Art* 2, No. 2 (1992): 1-5.

Miles, Jean. "Introduction." *Computers and the History of Art* 1, No. 1 (1990): 1-2.

Nyhan, Julianne, Andrew Flinn, and Anne Welsh. "Oral History and the Hidden Histories project: towards histories of computing in the humanities." *Digital Scholarship in the Humanities* 30, No. 1 (2015): 71-85.

Porter, Vicki and Robin Thomas. *A Guide to the Description of Architectural Drawings*. New York: G.K. Hall & Co., 1994.

Promey, Sally M. and Miriam Stewart. "Digital Art History: A New Field for Collaboration." *American Art* 11, No. 2 (1997): 36-41.

Vaughan, William. "The Automated Connoisseur: Image Analysis and Art History." In *History and Computing*, edited by Peter Denley and Deian Hopkin, 215-221. Manchester: Manchester University Press, 1987.

--- "Automated Picture Referencing: A Further look at 'Morelli'." *Computers and the History of Art* 2, No. 2 (1992): 7-18.

--- "Computergestützte Bildrecherche und Bildanalyse." In *Kunstgeschichte digital: eine Einführung für Praktiker und Studierende*, edited by Hubertus Kohle, 97-105. Berlin: Dietrich Reimer Verlag, 1997.

Zorich, Diane. *Transitioning to a Digital World: Art History, Its Research Centers, and Digital Scholarship.* New York: Samuel H. Kress Foundation, 2012.

--- "The "Art" of Digital Art History." Paper presented at the Index of Christian Art, Princeton University, June 26, 2013.

Benjamin Zweig, Ph.D., is the Robert H. Smith Postdoctoral Research Associate for Digital Art History at the Center for Advanced Study in the Visual Arts (CASVA) National Gallery of Art, Washington DC. He received his Ph.D. in Art History from Boston University. He is a medievalist by training, with a particular interest in digital mapping and developing/writing tools useful for art historical research.

Correspondence e-mail: b-zweig@nga.gov

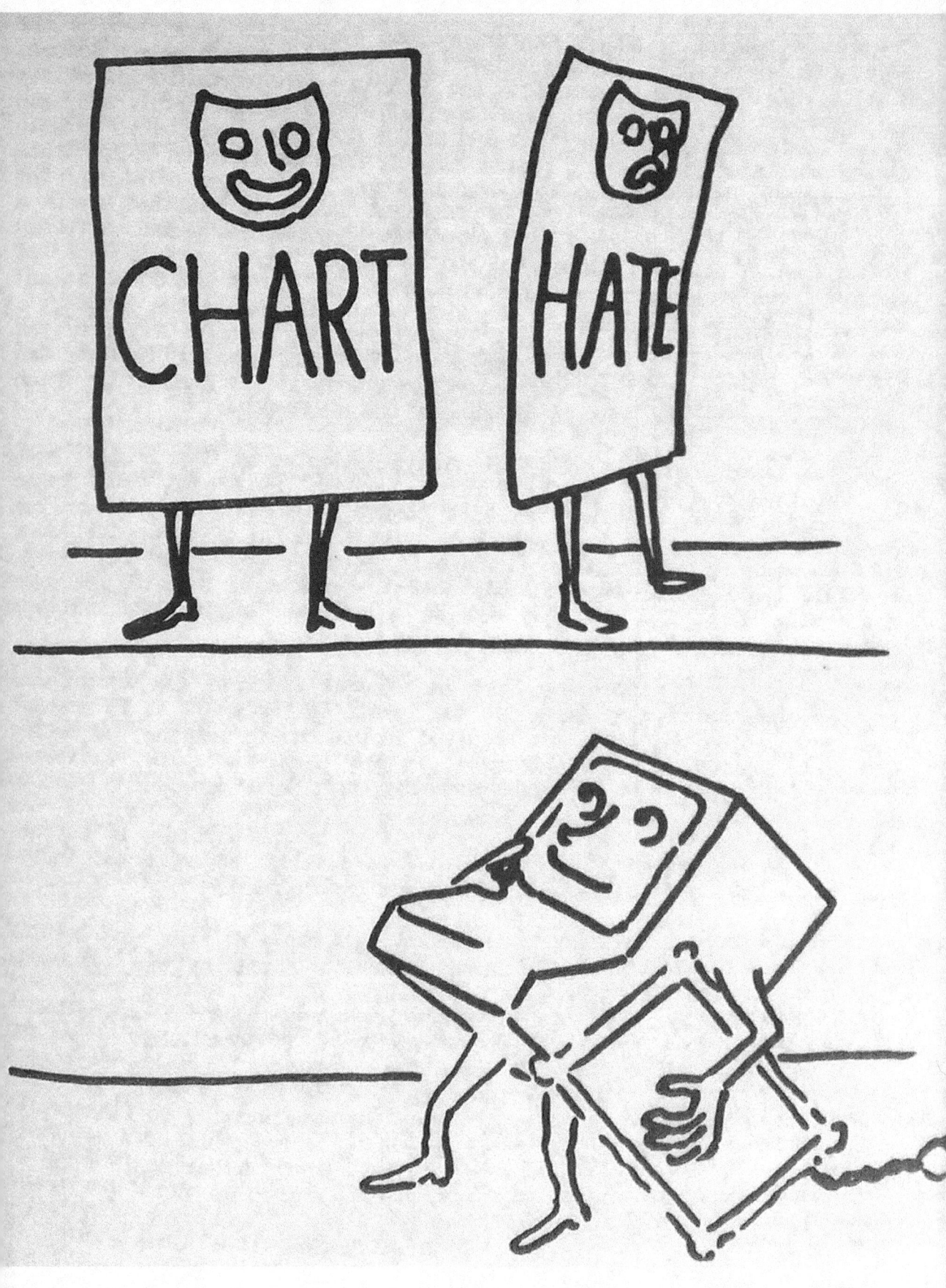

Invited Article
Debating Digital Art History

Anna Bentkowska-Kafel

Abstract: This paper offers a few reflections on the origins, historiography and condition of the field often referred to as Digital Art History (DAH), with references, among others, to the activities of the Computers and the History of Art group (CHArt, est. 1985) and my personal experience, spanning over 20 years, first as a postgraduate student, then doctoral researcher and eventually Lecturer in DAH. The publications and teaching activities of scholars connected to CHArt are seen as indicative of the evolution of the field internationally. Personal experience, or a reality check, is limited to higher education in the UK. The key argument here concerns the questionable benefit of promoting DAH as a discrete discipline and detaching digital practices from the mainstream history of art and its institutions. When introduced in the late 1990s, the 'DAH' served to indicate a dramatic shift in the way art history could be practiced, taught, studied and communicated. The changes were brought about by widening access to computers and information technology. DAH was suggested—"perhaps a little ahead of time—as a new kind of intellectual fusion" (W. Vaughan). It is no longer necessary to argue for the wise use of computers. Digital technology has become part and parcel of teaching, learning and research. It is the History of Art and its more traditional research methods and critical perspectives that are seen at risk of neglect. The theories of crisis, even 'death' of Art History have contributed to general anxiety over the discipline's future. However, a discipline has "the ability and power to control and judge its borders" (R. Nelson). The discipline of Art History is richer and stronger through the fusion of digital scholarship with, not separation, from more traditional methodologies and critical canons. The need to continue with the 'digital' distinction is questionable.

Keywords: art history, arts computing, digital art history, historiography

Digital Art History. A new or old field?[1]

HAIR – History of Art Information and Resources; HAGGIS – History of Art Group for Information Systems; and HACKS – History of Art, Computers, Knowledge, Slides, were among many names proposed in 1985 for a group, which eventually established itself internationally under the name of Computers and the History of Art, or CHArt.[2] The

Figure 1: A cartoon drawing by an unknown hand, in CHArt Newsletter, 2 (1986): 21.
(© CHArt. Reproduced by permission)

acronym CHIMERA was also considered, in the same light-hearted spirit, but was rejected on the grounds of 'enough anxieties about our ontological status already'.[3] Thirty years on, does this anxiety not sound familiar to those engaged in art-historical computing?

After a few years of intense activity and debate, in 1989 CHArt published its first scholarly overview of the field. The book was titled, predictably, *Computers and the History of Art*.[4] A bibliographic record, located in what appears an early online library catalogue, reads 'No discipline assigned' (Fig. 2). It shows the bibliographer's inability to assign the title to any discipline known at the time. Why the bibliographer did not classify this book under the History of Art, which features in the title, gives food for thought.

The present new Journal and numerous recent and upcoming international events are indicative of the renewed interest in Digital Art History (DAH).[5] Four institutes held in the US in the summer of 2014 led to the belief that 'Digital Art History Takes Off'.[6] This has been a frustratingly long 'take-off'. The tendency is to discuss and define this field through its presumed novelty and in opposition to art-historical scholarship and its dissemination formats that do not rely on digital media. Digital Humanities (DH) has been engaged in a similar debate. The blurred relationship between DAH and DH has been noted on many occasions. For example, in the *Digital Art History* workshop organized by the Getty Research Institute and the University of Málaga in 2011.[7] The resulting publication, with additional material, includes the burning question, on this occasion

Figure 2: Computers and the History of Art (1989) and the book record at http://www.getcited.org/pub/102797848 (accessed 1.03.2013).

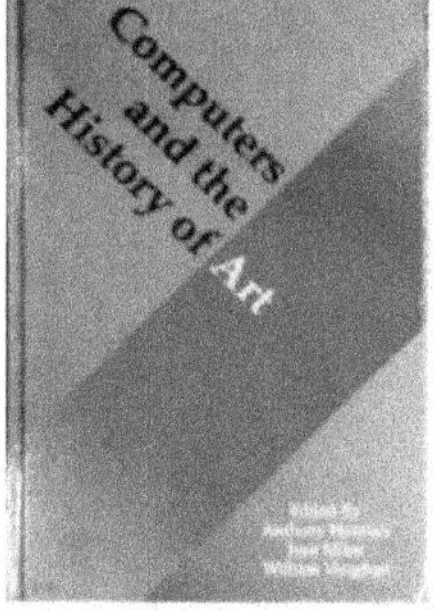

raised by Johanna Drucker, 'Is There a "Digital" Art History?'[8]

Why do we continue raising questions concerning the ontological status of DAH? Are we asking the wrong questions? Or, being engaged in this field in one way or another, are we simply asking for recognition? Those who are new to this debate, students in particular, may find this continued scrutiny of the place of digital technology in the art-historical practice and critical inquiry confusing and perhaps even pointless. These few personal reflections on the origins, historiography and condition of DAH are addressed to them.

Am I a Digital Humanist or a Digital Art Historian or, simply, an Art Historian?

The big question for this Journal—what is DAH?—has been recurring since the late 1990s. The desire to define the field anew has been the reason for convening the aforementioned recent international events. What it takes to become a digital art historian and pursue a career in this field is an interrelated question. In most disciplines the level of professionalism is normally determined by a degree or another recognized qual-ification after a period of training. If one practices medicine without a diploma, one is a charlatan; if one paints without having studied fine art, one is a dilettante. Is it necessary to have a degree in DAH to be considered a professional digital art historian?

In 1990 the Department of the History of Art at Birkbeck College, University of London, introduced an MA in Computer Applications for the History of Art, later renamed MA DAH. Postgraduate students were taught by the art historian William Vaughan, photography expert Anthony Hamber and art imaging scientist Kirk Martinez, among others. These academics were engaged at the time (1989–92) in the European Esprit II project, best known under the acronym VASARI — Visual Art System for Archiving and Retrieval of Images. The project was a collaboration between Birkbeck, the National Gallery in London, Bramuer Ltd. UK, Telecom Paris, the Doerner Institute in Munich and other institutions. Benefiting from the funding of around US$2 million, the project developed a prototype scanner and a methodological basis for accurate color reproduction of paintings, for the purpose of recording and conservation.

Apart from the expertise of the teachers and their infectious enthusiasm for computing, Birkbeck's students benefited from a departmental Vasari computer lab. It was well-equipped with *networked* Mac and IBM computers, a Silicon Graphics workstation for imaging and 3D work, scanners and a wide range of software. The syllabus could be envied by many Art History departments even today.[9] The emphasis was on critical discussion of the value of using computational methods in art-historical investigations. Essay/exam questions included, for example: 'To what extent have imaging techniques for pictorial analysis yielded *concrete results* for the study of art history?'; 'Discuss the value of using statistical methods in the study of history of art, using *specific examples.*' [my emphasis] Of course, to be able to answer such questions, it was mandatory for the student to have a background in art history, as well as acquire practical computing skills, including basic coding. I arrived at Birkbeck with a master's degree in 'straightforward' 'old' History of Art and several years of curatorial museum experience. The reading list drew on a considerable body of specialist literature published in the 1980s, with a significant number of titles published by CHArt and the Getty Art History Information Program (AHIP). The course is no longer offered.

Having graduated from Birkbeck in 1994, with an MA in Computer Applications for the History of Art, I went on to do a PhD in digital iconology. I located a small body of some 50 Early-Modern paintings, drawings and prints representing nature in human form. I undertook to establish, mainly through sixteenth- and seventeenth-century cosmological texts, the purpose and meaning of such anthropomorphic representations for the contemporary beholder. I was curious to find out why a number of mediocre artists depicted landscape as a human figure; how many such works have survived, in what form and where. I wanted to describe, classify, date and attribute these double images to particular schools and propose an indexing system independent of ambiguous subject classifications. I was also driven by a determination to prove a prominent critic of my chosen computational methods wrong. I owe him my gratitude. Every stage of my 'old-fashioned' research—pre-iconographical, iconographical and iconological—benefited from digital tools, computer graphics, pattern recognition and image processing in particular.[10]

In the course of my unconventional career I have had the opportunity to slowly, but steadily introduce classes in DAH. First, in 1995, to a BA (Hons) Art and Design History course at Southampton Institute, then to the graduate and postgraduate programs at Birkbeck and the Centre for Computing in the Humanities at King's College London. I renamed the King's module to Digital Arts and Culture, making it more approachable to students. In 2014–2015 it is being offered for the last time.

King's Digital Humanities has offered me a stimulating academic environment; a scholarly community of distinction with critical enthusiasm for arts computing. From 2000–2008 I also worked at the Courtauld Institute of Art on the British Academy's *Corpus of Romanesque Sculpture in Britain and Ireland*. Regrettably, there was no interest to embed this or any other large-scale computer-based projects, hosted by the Institute, in the teaching curricula, to enable students to learn from the then cutting-edge digitization practices. Project teams endeavored, in collaboration with external specialists, to produce digital images of medieval stain-glass and sculpture of the highest resolution possible, coded records of objects in XML, automated some of the editorial processes, designed databases and managed large sets of data[11], while postgraduate students and academics continued to rely on the slide library and print reproductions in the Conway and Witt libraries renowned for the custom-made, red and green filing boxes. The situation at King's Centre for Computing in the Humanities (now the Department of Digital Humanities) was quite the opposite. Postgraduate teaching has always evolved around scholarly computer-based projects, which established the reputation of the Department. This has been a computer-friendly environment, but my art-historical specialism, with its emphasis on visual arts, rather than text, felt out of place.

It was the recognition of digital visualization as a scholarly method of Digital Humanities that provided a welcome context to my research, and extended teaching and training opportunities to include historical visualization and virtual museums.[12] Through experimentation with digital tools and processes my students and I have been able to better understand the complexity of human perception. The opportunity to experience and discuss, for example, the potential cognitive value of machine haptics in simulating touch and handling of museum objects that is normally not possible, made us more aware of the extent to which art-historical appreciation and museum education privilege the role of visual experience (Fig. 3).

Despite benefiting from affiliation to DH, I believe the place of DAH is within academic art institutions, ideally with access to teaching art collections.

Digital Art History. A history

Art History has been described by Robert Nelson as "a discipline that typically studies the histories of everything but itself, conveniently forgetting that it, too, has a history and is History."[13]

An early use of the phrase 'DAH' is in 1997 by Sally M. Promey and Miriam Stewart in "Digital Art History: a new field for collaboration", published in *American Art.*[14] The authors describe teaching and learning with digital images, and recognize "the larger implications of new electronic technologies for visual education and scholarship in the museum and the academy".[15] There is no mention of DAH other than in the title, but the authors offer a number of insightful observations concerning the subject.

Since its initiation in 1985, CHArt "has set out to promote interaction between the rapidly developing new IT and the study and practice of Art. [Over the years] it has become increasingly clear that this interaction has led, not just to provision of new tools for carrying out of existing practices, but to the evolution of unprecedented activities and modes of thought. It was in recognition of this change that we decided, in 2001 to hold a conference entitled 'DAH' [*A Subject in Transition: Opportunities and Problems*], suggesting – perhaps a little ahead of time – a new kind of intellectual fusion."

explains William Vaughan.[16] The subject of the conference proved extremely controversial. Therefore, the following year CHArt convened, again at the British Academy, the conference *Digital Art History? Exploring Practice in a Network Society,* adding a question mark and the emphasis on the impact of the internet on art and AH.[17] CHArt's voice was international and far-ranging, but not unanimous in the understanding of DAH.

One may argue that the founding principles and methods of DAH were laid down decades ago. The vision and achievements of pioneers of arts computing deserve proper recognition. Some key concepts were developed well before the advent of personal computers and the internet, *in anticipation* of information communication technology as it is known today. "A worldwide museum information network for research, [...] lectures and simulated exhibitions (in audio/visual form) delivered electronically, upon request, to a classroom console or even to the home" was Everett Ellin's vision already in the mid-1960s.[18] Significant considerations and applications of computer technology—demonstrating its benefit to the study of art—go back to the 1980s. The second *Conference in Automatic Processing of Art History Data and Documents,* held in Pisa in 1984, set the international research agenda for years to come.[19] The need to learn programming languages seemed then inevitable and frightened most art historians, but not William Vaughan. In the 1980s he initiated the development of early pattern recognition software for matching and retrieval of images of paintings. Using the University of Cambridge (UK) mainframe computer, the architectural historian Tim Benton of the Open University created a database of Le Corbusier's architectural drawings and notes. He went on to enhance this resource with tools for scaling and comparing the drawings in a way not possible with paper originals.[20] The resource is not widely available, but the insights into the architect's creative

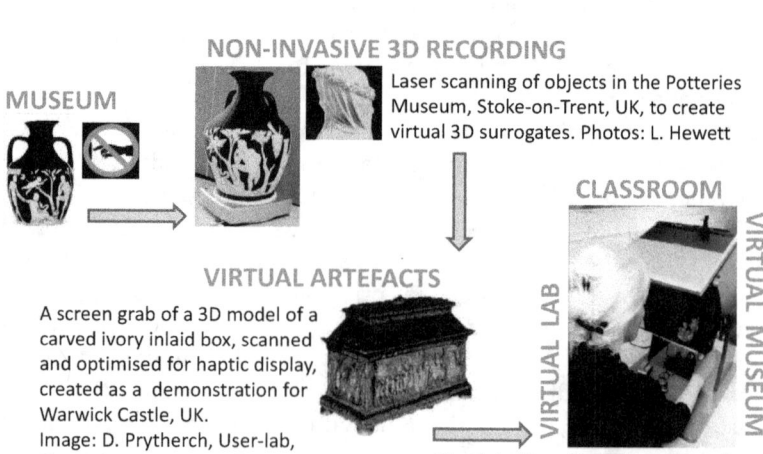

Figure 3: Understanding touch and its value in art studies; a postgraduate class taught by Anna Bentkowska-Kafel, King's College. London and David Prytherch, Birmingham Institute of Art and Design, 2009–2015.

A postgraduate course in Digital Arts and Culture, Department of Digital Humanities, King's College London, UK © Anna Bentkowska-Kafel and David Prytherch

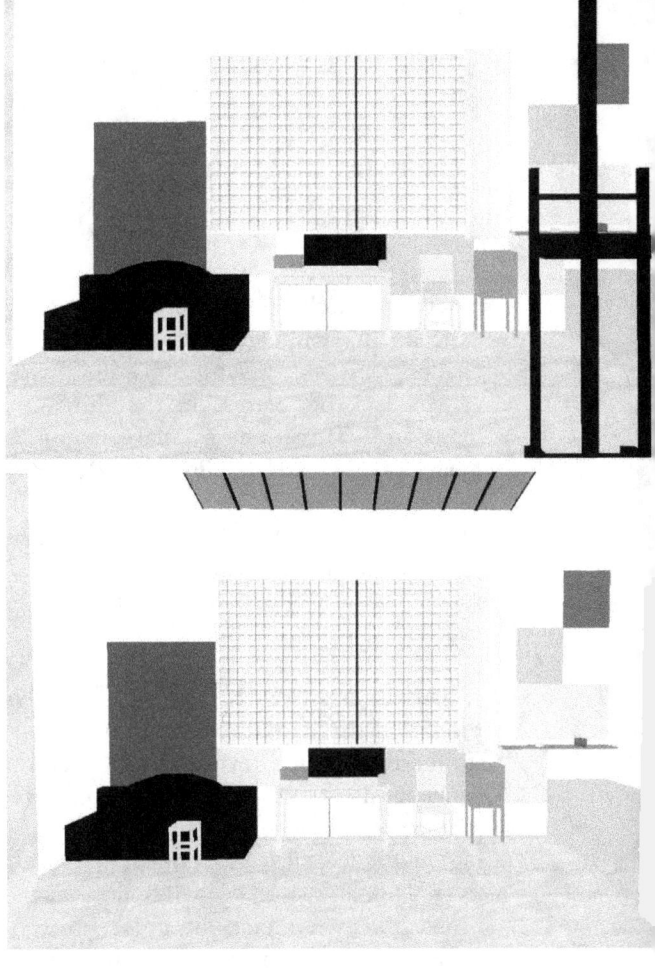

Figure 4: Visualization of Piet Mondrian's studio at 5 rue de Coulmiers, Paris. South wall view with and without easel.
(© Ryan Egel-Andrews, 2009)

process it has enabled are evidenced in Benton's writings. The pioneering work of Marilyn Aronberg Lavin in the course of her research into "the narrative disposition of medieval and Renaissance mural decoration", since 1988, involved the creation of a database of some 280 fresco cycles and construction of a computer model of the Cappella Maggiore of San Francesco in Arezzo, decorated with Piero della Francesca's the *Legend of the True Cross*.[21] A later version of the 3D model is, remarkably, still available online.[22]

When we talk about the nature and significance of DAH, we recognize the rise in the status of this field. Some of the earlier concerns over Art History "not being at the helm of the sweeping visualization revolution" have been resolved, although not entirely satisfactorily.[23]

However, defining the nature of DAH, in all its cognitive and methodological complexity, proves more difficult. It is relatively straightforward to look at the applications of digital technology—past and current—to art practice, art scholarship, conservation and education. They give us a good picture how the field has evolved over the years, and help to foresee its possible future directions. Whether applied DAH has led to establishing a theoretical basis that could set the field firmly *within* or *apart* from mainstream AH is an open question. There is no area of DAH that cognitively would be distinct from AH. Evolving digital analytical methods facilitate the discovery of new knowledge and review of earlier scholarship. It is particularly satisfying when this discovery comes from students, as in the case of Ryan Egel-Andrews's original, visualization-based research into Piet Mondrian's experiments with architectural space. It challenges earlier assumptions about the artist's lack of interest in the third dimension.[24] Three-dimensional computer model of the artist studio supported the reading of Mondrian's writings and interpretation of Neoplastic principles. A photo-realistic recreation of architectural space was not the aim of this visualization.

Digital Art History has been mainly promoted through applications of digital technology. Little effort has been made to conceptualize this practice; to connect projects and evaluate patterns in emerging methodologies and critical perspectives. Digital Art History has not established its own canon of critical texts. When asked to identify the most significant written works about New Media art 1970–2000, Lev Manovich proposed a list of ten titles.[25] Literature on applied DAH is abounding, but I would find it difficult to identify critical texts that have made a lasting impact.

Reconnecting Digital Art History to Art History

In the introduction to his popular anthology of critical texts in *Art History and its Methods* (1st ed. 1995), Eric Fernie refutes the apparent 'death' of Art History.[26] He addresses a need to present a history of the methods, "which art historians have found appropriate or productive in studying the objects and ideas which constitute their discipline [believing that] undergraduates might welcome a discussion of the range of approaches available to them for the study of their subject [...]".[27] When referring to the present, Fernie notes 'Versatility and Potential'. There is no mention of the computer. No text concerning its use or impact on key concepts is included in the anthology. While the addition of digital practice and more recent texts would be welcome in future editions (similarly to the anthology edited by Donald Preziosi[28]), my identification of the lack of theoretical writings concerned explicitly with DAH is not a criticism.

In his keynote address to the first CHArt conference dedicated to DAH, held in 2001, Eric Fernie was not only provocative, but also right to question the very concept of DAH as a subject separate from the traditional History of Art.[29] DAH scholarship has investigated intrinsically 'mainstream' art-historical questions, such as the narrative schemes in Italian Renaissance wall decoration, and artistic principles of Mondrian's Neoplasticism. Digital iconology needs Panofsky. The study of digital aesthetics would be poorer without Kant or Goodman. A phenomenological critique of virtual historical environments may only benefit from the writings of Wilhelm Dilthey. Walter Benjamin's *The Work of Art in the Age of Mechanical Reproduction* [1936] is probably one of the most frequently cited texts in discussions of digital culture. Critical perspectives of DAH are well served by a much broader canon.

Art History has always been interdisciplinary and always aware of broader theoretical contexts. Serious art-historical arguments not only require, but necessitate erudite knowledge of—variably—history of ideas, philosophy, history, literature, religion and beliefs, etc. Earlier attempts at defining DAH have been only partly successful, because they sought the differences rather than affinities with established methodologies and conventions. It is impossible to address art-historical questions—whether philosophical, social, political, formal and aesthetical—without drawing on the history of human thought and artistic practice. Digital research into art and cultural heritage, which has not been informed by a professional art-historical knowledge and rigorous scholarly methodology, often demonstrates inferior or uncertain cognitive value of the findings. Examples include historical visualization that does not show the difference between known facts and hypotheses.

Digital Art History is not a discrete discipline, but an umbrella name for methods that involve digital tools, techniques and processes of analysis and interpretation, ranging from basic statistics to complex applications of Artificial Intelligence (computer vision, pattern recognition, automation, etc.). These tools and techniques are not unique to Art History; they are uni-methods. The Zurich Declaration on Digital Art History (2014) reads like recommendations for digital scholarship in general.[30] Its eight points—on methodology, authority data, archives and collections, big data, digital workspace, open access, legal matters and sustainability—describe the conditions that are necessary to practice many other disciplines.

Like 'New Media' and 'Digital Humanities', 'DAH' is a temporary name that has served its purpose. By continuing to emphasize the 'digital', rather than

Figure 5: Students of Digital Arts and Culture at Michael Takeo Magruder's *De/Coding the Apocalypse* exhibition, Somerset House, King's College London. (Photo: A. Bentkowska-Kafel, 2014)

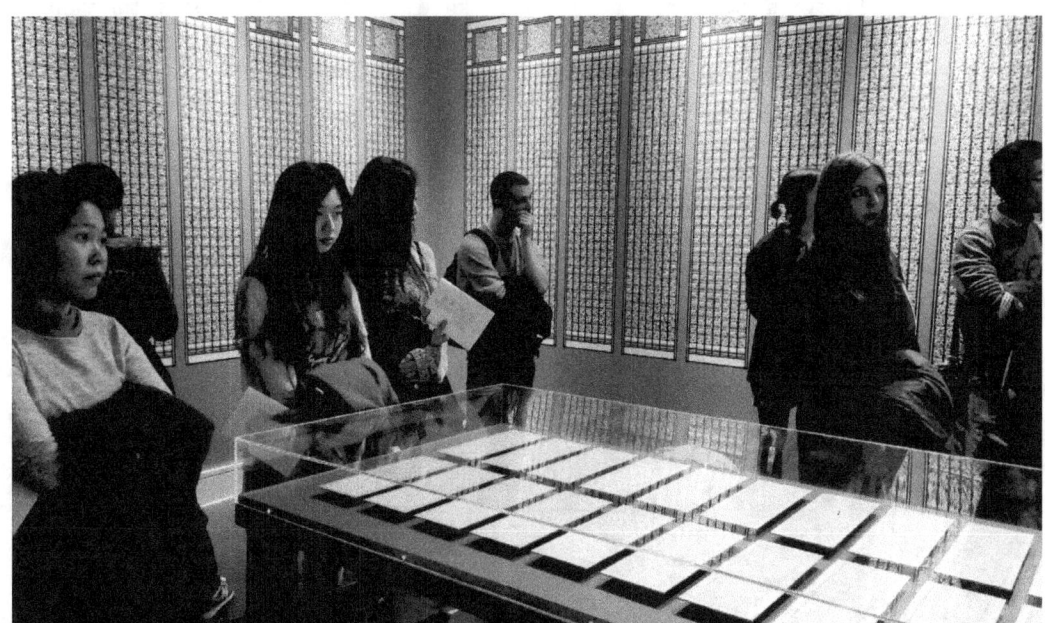

'art' and 'history', we are contributing to further ontological disruption of the discipline. We should instead stress the significance of earlier thought and methods.

Hans Belting believed that "Both the artist and the art historian have lost faith in a rational, teleological process of artistic history, a process to be carried out by the one and described by the other".[31] The twentieth-century rift between art-historical scholarship and art practice (about which Belting argued so eloquently, if controversially) is alleviated when an art form is also a means of scholarly inquiry. The *De/Coding the Apocalypse* exhibition (Somerset House, 2014) may serve as an example of art, which has the power of reconnecting artistic practice with scholarly enquiry and learning.[32] This particular collaboration was between the computer artist, Michael Takeo Magruder, programming and digital technology specialists, and theology scholars. Visiting the exhibition has inspired the students of Digital Arts and Culture to decode the Book of Revelation of St John the Divine and interpret it for their own time.

According to critics, the crisis of academic art history is partly due to changing education needs and students' loss of interest in historical art; the tendency to ignore historical sources; increasing neglect of fieldwork and archival research; "denigration of critical thinking as practiced in the pre-digital age".[33] It is therefore counter-productive to continue to differentiate between DAH and AH. The emphasis should be on erudite historical knowledge, including earlier digital scholarship and its historiography. Art, rather than application of digital technology, should be seen as the incentive for acquiring this knowledge. DAH should drop the 'Digital' label which soon will become irrelevant anyway. The embrace of digital technology in the best possible manner and in *intellectual fusion*, not in opposition to critical and methodological traditions of the discipline, is a way of demonstrating that there is no 'crisis', no 'lagging behind', that continues to plague the reputation of the academic history of art and is discouraging new students.

Students are interested in history when it is presented as relevant and in a way they find appealing. The classroom-based model of teaching, with the typical projection of images of art, away from art being the subject of study, is now an inferior mode of teaching and learning. Although not without logistical problems, a class at the *De/Coding Apocalypse* exhibition, led by the artist, is a perfect scenario. Students responded with equal enthusiasm, and eagerness to learn, when they visited the National Gallery, London to study Hans Holbein the Younger's so-called *Ambassadors* (1533), in the vicinity of other works of the artist and best examples of Western painting.

"What would be a digital modern equivalent to the Holbein image?"—is a question that in the early days of my teaching career I would not have asked of postgraduate students. Today such a question inspires international students of the Google and Wikipedia generation to learn about the making, meaning and provenance of Holbein's masterpiece; the art, music, science, religion and politics of the time. The students typically represent different cultural backgrounds and very different levels of general knowledge; some are unfamiliar with European Renaissance. In the case under discussion, the inspiration to learn history *and* digital technology came primarily from the sixteenth-century work of art. The digital collage that resulted from student collaboration was based on a thorough study of sources, surprisingly also books in print. The collage employed a variety of media, including an original musical composition. It was creative and funny, but also thoughtful and critical of the past and present. The students also learned about copyright restrictions that are preventing a public showing of their coursework. The future of the History of Art is in training of the observant eye and knowledgeable, critical mind, using digital tools when useful. CHArt's early idea of HACKS requires only one revision—History of Art, Computers, Knowledge, *seriously*.

Notes

[1] Acknowledgements: I wish to thank the Editors of the *International Journal for Digital Art History*, Harald Klinke and Liska Surkemper, for the invitation to share these comments with the readers of the first issue of their Journal. I am grateful to the Editors and Trish Cashen, Neil Grindley, Hubertus Kohle and Jeremy Pilcher for reading the manuscript and for their excellent critical comments. The paper is partly based on my unpublished talk, *Mapping Digital Art History*. The missing chapter, presented to the Digital Art History Laboratory at the Getty Research Institute, CA, held 5–8 March 2013.

[2] See Computers and the History of Art (CHArt), www.chart.ac.uk. All URLs active on 15 April 2015, unless stated otherwise.

[3] Dave Guppy, Will Vaughan and Charles Ford, eds., *Computers and the History of Art Newsletter*, 1 (1985): 26.

[4] Anthony Hamber, Jean Miles and William Vaughan, eds., *Computers and the History of Art* (London and New York: Mansell Pub., 1989).

[5] For example, *Digital Art History*, Mellon Research Initiative, convened by Jim Coddington at the Institute of Fine Arts, New York University, 30 November – 1 December 2012; http://www.nyu.edu/gsas/dept/fineart/research/mellon/mellon-digital.htm; *Digital Art History Laboratory* held at the Getty Research Institute, CA, 5–8 March 2013; *Digital Art History: Challenges and Prospects*, International Conference, held at the Swiss Institute for Art Research (SIK-ISEA), Zürich, 26–27 June 2014; http://www.gta.arch.ethz.ch/events/digital-art-history-challenges-and-prospects.

[6] Anne Collins Goodyear and Paul B. Jaskot, "Digital Art History takes off", *CAA News*, College Art Association, 7 October 2014, http://www.collegeart.org/news/2014/10/07/digital-art-history-takes-off/

[7] *Digital Art History: Challenges, Tools & Practical Solutions*, University of Málaga and the Getty Research Institute (GRI), Malaga, 19–22 September 2011, http:/digitalarthistory.weebly.com/

[8] *Visual Resources. An International Journal of Documentation*, Special Issue on Digital Art History edited by Murtha Baca *et al.*, 29.1 (2013). J. Drucker's opening article, 'Is There a "Digital" Art History?', 5–13.

[9] Anthony Hamber, "Computer Applications in the History of Art. A Perspective from Birkbeck College, University of London", in *La Revue Informatique et Statistique dans les Sciences Humaines*, Université de Liège, 29.1–4 (1992): 86–89.

[10] Anna Bentkowska, "Computer-aided Iconological Analysis of Anthropomorphic Landscapes in Western Art, c. 1560-1660" (doctoral thesis; multimedia CD-ROM, Nottingham Trent University, 1998); "Ikonologia cyfrowa – nowe oblicze starej metody" [English summary: 'Digital Iconology. A New Approach to the Old Method'], in *Ars Longa*, published in memory of Professor Jan Białostocki, ed. Teresa Hrankowska (Warsaw: Arx Regia, 1999), 387–409.

[11] Anna Bentkowska-Kafel, "Electronic Corpora of Artefacts: The Example of the Corpus of Romanesque Sculpture in Britain and Ireland", in *The Virtual Representation of the Past*, eds. Mark Greengrass and Lorna Hughes (Farnham: Ashgate, 2008), 179–190.

[12] Martyn Jessop, "*Visualization as a Scholarly*

Activity", Literary and Linguistic Computing, 23, no. 3 (2008): 281–93. Anna Bentkowska-Kafel, "'*I bought a piece of Roman furniture on the Internet. It's quite good but low on polygons*'—Digital Visualization of Cultural Heritage and its Scholarly Value in Art History," *Visual Resources. An International Journal of Documentation*, Special Issue on Digital Art History ed. Murtha Baca *et al.*, 29, no. 1 (2013): 38–46.

[13] Robert S. Nelson, "The Map of Art History", *The Art Bulletin*, 79, no. 1 (1997): 28.

[14] Sally M. Promey and Miriam Stewart, "Digital Art History: a new field for collaboration", *American Art*, 11, no. 2 (1997): 36–41.

[15] Ibid, 36.

[16] William Vaughan, "Introduction. Digital Art History?", in *Digital Art History – A Subject in Transition*, ed. Anna Bentkowska-Kafel, Trish Cashen and Hazel Gardiner (Bristol and Portland: Intellect, 2005), 1.

[17] The programmes for both conferences are available at http://www.chart.ac.uk/chart01programme.html and http://www.chart.ac.uk/cfp2002.html respectively. Selected papers have been published in two volumes of proceedings online and in book format, op. cit., note 15 above.

[18] Everett Ellin, "Museums and the computer. An Appraisal of new potentials," *Computers and the Humanities* 4 *(1969)*: 25–30.

[19] Laura Corti and Marilyn Schmitt, eds., *International Conference in Automatic Processing of Art History Data and Documents*, held at the Scuola Superiore de Pisa, 24–27 Sept 1984, Scuola Superiore de Pisa and the Getty Trust AHIP, Santa Monica (1984). The Conference was first held in 1978.

[20] Tim Benton, "Le Corbusier and his drawings: an integrated database and drawing package". Abstract of paper presented to *Digital Environments: Design, Heritage and Architecture*, Fifteenth Annual Conference of Computers and the History of Art, 24–25 September 1999, University of Glasgow, available at http://www.chart.ac.uk/chart99/benton.html

[21] I wish to thank Marilyn Aronberg Lavin for clarifying the nature and scope of her collaborative computing work; the citation is to email communication of 14 Jan 2013; see her "Piero della Francesca: Legend of the True Cross: 3-D Walkthrough, Realtime, Interactive Computer Model", *1492. Rivista della Fondazione Piero della Francesca* 1 (2009): 59–72, revised in http://www.archimuse.com/mw2009/

[22] http://projects.ias.edu/pierotruecross

[23] Barbara Maria Stafford in: Kathleen Cohen, James Elkins, Marilyn Aronberg Lavin et al., "Digital Culture and the Practices of Art and Art History." *Art Bulletin* 79, no. 2 (1997): 214.

[24] Ryan Egel-Andrews, "Paradata in Art-historical Research. A Visualization of Piet Mondrian's Studio at 5 rue de Coulmiers", in *Paradata and Transparency in Virtual Heritage*, ed. Anna Bentkowska-Kafel and Hugh Denard (Farnham: Ashgate, 2012): 109–124. Abstract at https://visualizationparadata.wordpress.com/10-2/

[25] Lev Manovich, "Ten Key Texts on Digital Art: 1970–2000," *Leonardo* 35, no. 5 (2002): 567–569 and 571–575, also available at http://manovich.net/index.php/projects/key-texts-on-new-media-art

[26] *Art History and its Methods, a critical anthology*, Selection and commentary by Eric Fernie (London: Phaidon, 1995).

[27] Ibidem, 8.

[28] Donald Preziosi, ed., *The Art of Art History: A Critical Anthology* (Oxford University Press, 1998).

[29] Eric Fernie's keynote address has not been published. See, Anna Bentkowska-Kafel, Editorial, *Digital Art History – A Subject in Transition: Opportunities and Problems*, CHArt Conference Proceedings Online, 4 (2001), http://www.chart.ac.uk/chart2001/papers/noframes/editorial.html

[30] Zürich Declaration on Digital Art History (2014), http://www.gta.arch.ethz.ch/events/digital-art-history-challenges-and-prospects

[31] Hans Belting, *The End of the History of Art?* [1984], trans. Christopher S. Wood (Chicago and London: The University of Chicago Press, 1987): ix.

[32] Argula Rublack, "Exploring theology with digital art." A student review of the De/Coding the Apocalypse exhibition, based on postgraduate coursework, *Cassone. The Internatioal Online Magazine of Art and Art Books*, April 2015, http://www.cassone-art.com/magazine/article/2015/04/exploring-theology-with-digital-art/?psrc=photography-and-media

[33] Patricia Mainardi, "The Crisis in Art History. Introduction." *Visual Resources: An International Journal of Documentation* 27, no. 4 (2011): 303. Maxwell L. Anderson, "The Crisis in Art History: Ten Problems, Ten Solutions." ibidem, 337. Similar findings in Diane M. Zorich, *Transitioning to a Digital World. Art History, Its Research Centers, and Digital Scholarship*, A Report to the Samuel H. Kress Foundation and the Roy Rosenzweig Center

for History and New Media, George Mason University (2012), available at http://www.kress foundation.org/uploadedFiles/Sponsored_Research/Research/Zorich_TransitioningDigitalWorld.pdf

Bibliography

Anderson, Maxwell L. "The Crisis in Art History: Ten Problems, Ten Solutions." *Visual Resources. An International Journal of Documentation* 27, no. 4 (2011): 336–343.

Aronberg Lavin, Marilyn. "Piero della Francesca: Legend of the True Cross: 3-D Walkthrough, Realtime, Interactive Computer Model", in *1492. Rivista della Fondazione Piero della Francesca*, 1 (2009): 59–72, revised in http://www.archimuse.com/mw2009/

Belting, Hans. *The End of the History of Art?* [1984] Translated by Christopher S. Wood. Chicago and London: The University of Chicago Press, 1987.

Bentkowska, Anna. "Computer-aided Iconological Analysis of Anthropomorphic Landscapes in Western Art, c. 1560-1660." Doctoral thesis; multimedia CD-ROM, Nottingham Trent University, 1998.

Bentkowska, Anna. "Ikonologia cyfrowa – nowe oblicze starej metody" [English summary: 'Digital Iconology. A New Approach to the Old Method']. In *Ars Longa*, published in memory of Professor Jan Białostocki, edited by Teresa Hrankowska, 387–409. Warsaw: Arx Regia, 1999.

Bentkowska-Kafel, Anna. "Electronic Corpora of Artefacts: The Example of the Corpus of Romanesque Sculpture in Britain and Ireland.", In *The Virtual Representation of the Past*, edited by Mark Greengrass and Lorna Hughes, 179–190. Farnham: Ashgate 2008.

Bentkowska-Kafel, Anna. *"I bought a piece of Roman furniture on the Internet. It's quite good but low on polygons'*—Digital Visualization of Cultural Heritage and its Scholarly Value in Art History." *Visual Resources. An International Journal of Documentation*, Special Issue on Digital Art History edited by Murtha Baca et al., 29, no. 1 (2013): 38–46.

Cohen, Kathleen, James Elkins, Marilyn Aronberg Lavin, Barbara Maria Stafford et al., "Digital Culture and the Practices of Art and Art History." *Art Bulletin* 79, no. 2 (1997): 214.

Collins Goodyear, Anne and Paul B. Jaskot, "Digital Art History takes off", *CAA News*, College Art Association, 7 October 2014, http://www.collegeart.org/news/2014/10/07/digital-art-history-takes-off/

Corti, Laura and Marilyn Schmitt, eds. *International Conference in Automatic Processing of Art History Data and Documents*, held at the Scuola Superiore de Pisa, 24–27 Sept 1984. Scuola Superiore de Pisa and the Getty Trust AHIP, Santa Monica, 1984.

Drucker, Johanna. "Is There a 'Digital' Art History?", *Visual Resources. An International Journal of Documentation*, Special Issue on Digital Art History. Murtha Baca et al. eds., 29.1 (2013): 5–13.

Egel-Andrews, Ryan. "Paradata in Art-historical Research. A Visualization of Piet Mondrian's Studio at 5 rue de Coulmiers." In *Paradata and Transparency in Virtual Heritage*, edited by Anna Bentkowska-Kafel and Hugh Denard, 109–124. Farnham: Ashgate, 2012.

Ellin, Everett, *"*Museums and the computer. An Appraisal of new potentials.*"* *Computers and the Humanities* 4 (*1969):* 25–30.

Fernie, Eric, ed. *Art History and its Methods, a critical anthology.* London: Phaidon, 1995.

Guppy, Dave, Will Vaughan and Charles Ford, eds., *Computers and the History of Art Newsletter*, 1 (1985): 26.

Hamber, Anthony, Jean Miles and William Vaughan, eds. *Computers and the History of Art.* London and New York: Mansell Pub., 1989.

Hamber, Anthony. "Computer Applications in the History of Art. A Perspective from Birkbeck College, University of London." *La Revue Informatique et Statistique dans les Sciences Humaines*, Université de Liège, 29.1–4 (1992): 86–89.

Jessop, Martyn. *"Visualization as a Scholarly Activity."* *Literary and Linguistic Computing*, 23, no. 3 (2008): 281–93.

Mainardi, Patricia. "The Crisis in Art History. Introduction." *Visual Resources. An International Journal of Documentation* 27, no. 4 (2011): 303–305.

Manovich, Lev. "Ten Key Texts on Digital Art: 1970–2000." *Leonardo* 35, no. 5 (2002): 567–569 and 571–575, also available at http://manovich.net/index.php/projects/key-texts-on-new-media-art

Nelson, Robert S. "The Map of Art History." *The Art Bulletin*, 79, no. 1 (1997): 28.

Preziosi, Donald, ed. *The Art of Art History: A Critical Anthology.* Oxford University Press, 1998.

Promey, Sally M. and Miriam Stewart. "Digital Art History: a new field for collaboration." *American Art,* 11, no. 2 (1997): 36–41.

Rublack, Argula. "Exploring theology with digital art." Review of Michael Takeo Magruder's exhibition, De/Coding the Apocalypse. *Cassone. The Internatioal Online Magazine of Art and Art Books,* April 2015, http://www.cassone-art.com/magazine/article/2015/04/exploring-theology-with-digital-art/?psrc=photography-and-media

Vaughan, William. "Introduction. Digital Art History?" In *Digital Art History – A Subject in Transition,* edited by Anna Bentkowska-Kafel, Trish Cashen and Hazel Gardiner, 1–2. Bristol and Portland: Intellect, 2005.

Zorich, Diane M. *Transitioning to a Digital World. Art History, Its Research Centers, and Digital Scholarship,* A Report to the Samuel H. Kress Foundation and the Roy Rosenzweig Center for History and New Media, George Mason University (2012), available at http://www.kressfoundation.org/uploadedFiles/Sponsored_Research/Research/Zorich_TransitioningDigitalWorld.pdf

Zürich Declaration on Digital Art History (2014), http://www.gta.arch.ethz.ch/events/digital-art-history-challenges-and-prospects

Selected Websites (accessed 15 April 2015)

Computers and the History of Art (CHArt), www.chart.ac.uk

Digital Art History Challenges, Tools & Practical Solutions, University of Málaga and the Getty Research Institute (GRI), Malaga, 19–22 September 2011, http://digitalarthistory.weebly.com/

Digital Art History, Mellon Research Initiative convened by Jim Coddington at the Institute of Fine Arts, New York University, 30 November – 1 December 2012; http://www.nyu.edu/gsas/dept/fineart/research/mellon/mellon-digital.htm

Digital Art History Laboratory held at the Getty Research Institute, CA, 5–8 March 2013, http://digitalarthistory.weebly.com/agenda.html

Digital Art History: Challenges and Prospects, International Conference, held at the Swiss Institute for Art Research (SIK-ISEA), Zürich, 26–27 June 2014; http://www.gta.arch.ethz.ch/events/digital-art-history-challenges-and-prospects

Piero della Francesca: Legend of the True Cross. San Francesco, Arezzo, Italy: 3D Computer Model, http://projects.ias.edu/pierotruecross

Anna Bentkowska-Kafel is an independent scholar and part-time Lecturer in Digital Art History in the Department of Digital Humanities, King's College London, UK. She has been a longstanding committee member and editor for Computers and the History of Art (CHArt, est. 1985). She co-organized two CHArt conferences on Digital Art History held at the British Academy in 2001 and 2002, and co-edited the proceedings published by Intellect.

Correspondence e-mail: anna.bentkowska@kcl.ac.uk
bentkowska.wordpress.com

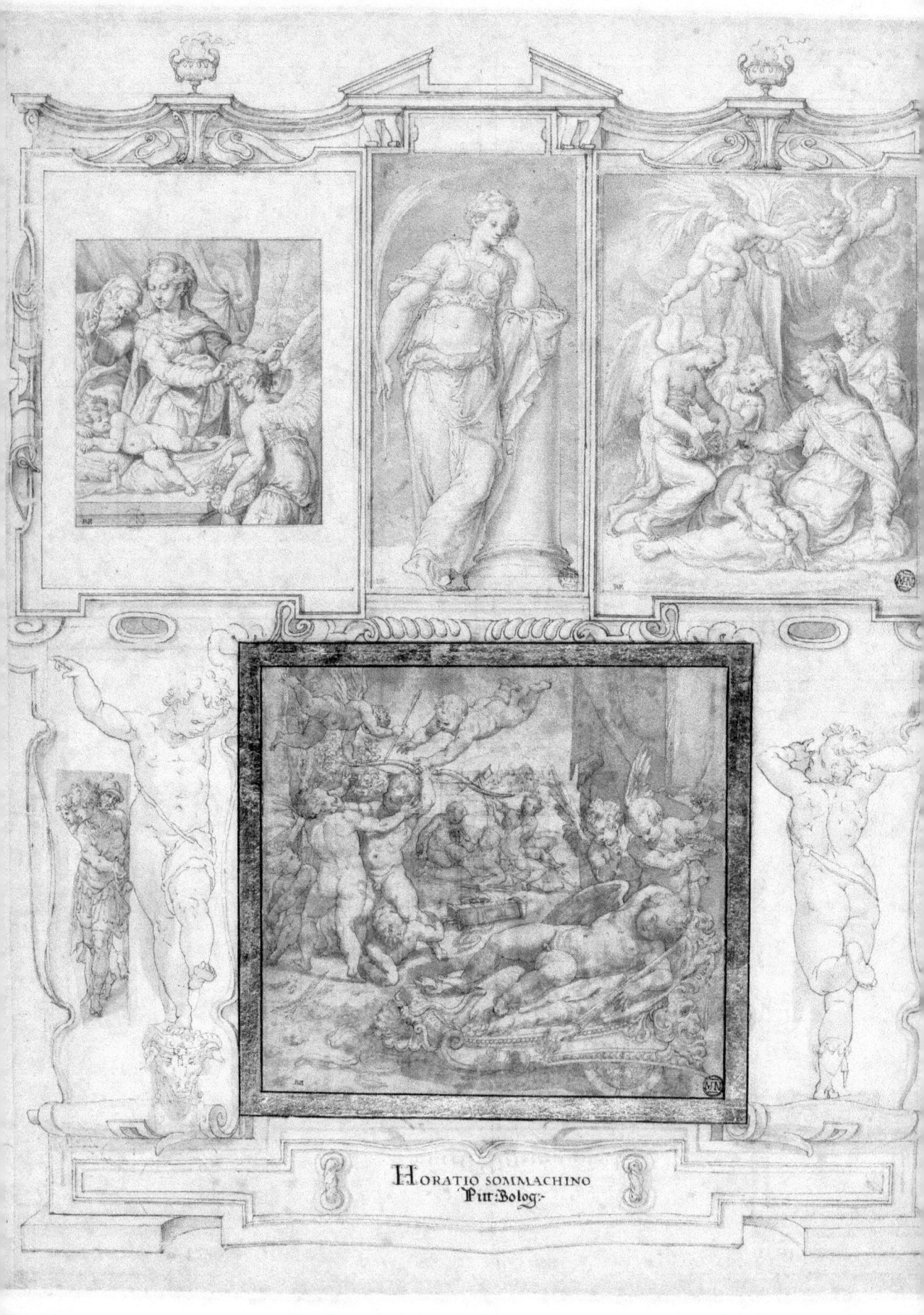

HORATIO SOMMACHINO
Pitt: Bolog:

Peer-Reviewed
Reframing Art History

Elli Doulkaridou

Abstract: Taking into account the call of this journal to examine the epistemological and methodological assumptions in the field of art history on the verge of its digital turn, the aim of this essay is to contribute to the ongoing discussion by questioning the role of the framing device in the context of image appropriation and critical interpretation of visual documents. Focusing on the cognitive and structural potential of the frame, a common feature between analogue and digital art historical practice, we try to provide points of historical perspective through a selection of particular examples (Giorgio Vasari, Gustav Ludwig and Aby Warburg) and bring them closer to the notions of instrumentation and interface.

Keywords: art historical methodologies, interface, frame theory, image manipulation, critical visual thinking, visual perception

Introduction

Digital Art History is "taking off." Summer institutes, conferences as well as new resources such as this journal, are emerging at an ever increasing rate.[1] Critical epistemological consciousness begins to morph and the study of visual forms of knowledge production makes room for the act of interpretation, more common in the humanist realm than in the natural sciences.

In his classic essay "Art History as a Humanistic Discipline" Erwin Panofsky posed the question: "How, then, is it possible to build up art history as a respectable scholarly discipline, if its very objects come into being by an irrational and subjective process?" His answer was, in part: "This question cannot be answered, of course, by referring to the scientific methods which have been, or may be, introduced into art history. Devices such as chemical analysis of materials, X-rays, ultraviolet rays, infrared rays and macrophotography are very helpful, but their use has nothing to do with the basic methodical problem. [...] These devices enable the art historian to see more than he

Figure 1: Orazio Samacchini (1532-1577), leaf from the *Libro de' Disegni*.
Paris, Musée du Louvre, D.A.G. INV 9024-recto.
(Photo: © RMN-Grand Palais (musée du Louvre) / Thierry Le Mage)

could see without them, but *what he sees* has to be interpreted 'stylistically', like that which he perceives with the naked eye."[2] What interests me here is not Panofsky's method *per se*, nor the many more that have followed; it is rather the juxtaposition of the instruments and of the act of interpretation. For Panofsky (as for many others), the art historian is a person with an equipped eye who interprets works of art.

In Panofsky's essay, which aimed primarily to define the humanistic underpinnings of a then very young discipline, this takes the form of a theoretical analysis. But there are also practical facets of that act of interpretation. Panofsky uses the terms "re-creation" and "archaeology of patterns", which he argues, constantly interpenetrate and nourish each other organically; today we could use the more generic terms "appropriation" and "critical interpretation". In both of these activities/phases of research, the role of the framing device seems crucial. What happens to this device in the digital sphere when it comes to art historical interpretative practice? I will try to provide some answers below, but first let us take a step back and approach our question historically.

In her 2010 article "Graphesis," Johanna Drucker stated that: "When it comes to using visualization as interpretation, [...] our practice is just beginning to take shape."[3] Her recent book, bearing the same title, provides a comprehensive overview and extremely suggestive ob-

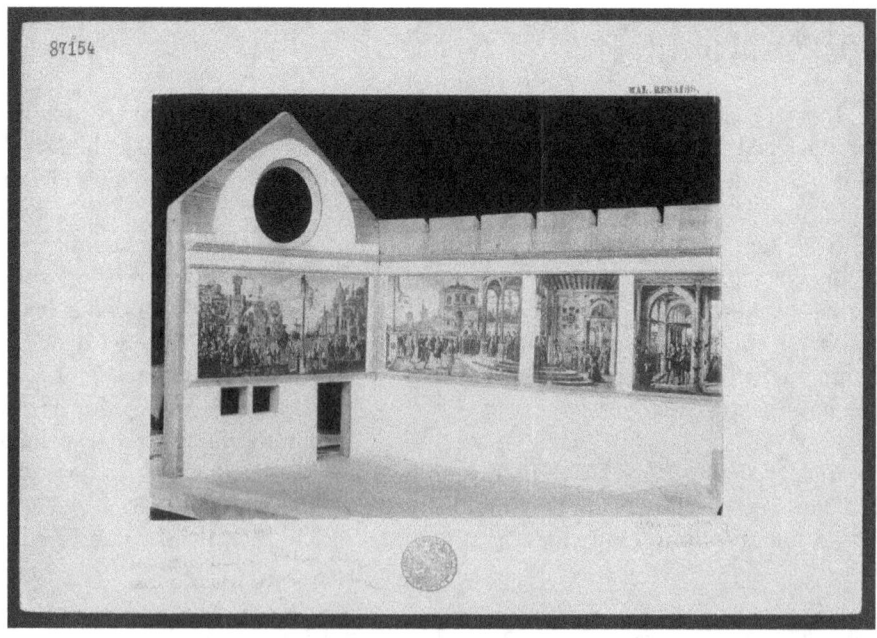

servations about the critical thinking of humanistic interfaces.[4] Instructively, the framing device emerges once again as a basic but nonetheless powerful structure, one that takes on new dimensions in the digital arena. Art history, however, is only briefly discussed in the scope of her essay, and I hope to contribute to the discussion by shedding light specifically on art historical practices pertaining to the use of the framing device.[5] The reflections that follow are the result of two converging interests and strands of research, the common denominator of which is the *framing device*. One is early modern decorative systems (such as the Sistine chapel ceiling) and the other is the use of the image as document by art historians.

I approach this topic through particular examples of art historical practice – some familiar if not indeed canonical, others less well-known. In adopting this line of reasoning, I take into account the recent call to examine our epistemological and methodological assumptions.[6] At the same time, I seek to bridge analog and digital art history by highlighting examples taken from the history of the field where one can observe elements of syntax, interpretation and subjectivity. My aim is to provide an alternative reading of art historical practices pertaining to image appropriation and interpretation, a reading that will shed both light on the notions of instrumentation and interface and provide points of historical perspective that might inspire the creation of more meaningful resources that will resonate with art historians.

The Framing Device as Element of Syntax and Cognition in Art Historical Practice

The notion of the "framing device" is essential and should not be dismissed casually.[7] For the present discussion, the "frame" is considered as a cognitive and structural element from the angle of visual semiotics. The frame has a functional value since it shows/ presents/ indicates – it is a sign of the index family,[8] and provides the conditions of contemplation and critical reception of the object shown.[9] In other words, it is an instrument of cognitive perception that encourages the articulation of visual elements and their appropriation by the viewer. But at the same time, when integrated within a system – or a complex visual environment such as a digital resource user interface (UI) – the frame becomes a nodal element. In other words, without shedding its previous qualities the frame further enables a network of

Figure 2: Probably Tomaso Filippi (photographer), *Reconstruction of Carpaccio's Sant'Orsola cycle with wooden model*, albumen print, c. 1904.
Photothek of the Kunsthistorisches Institut in Florenz, inv. 87154.
(Photo: © Photothek des Kunsthistorischen Instituts in Florenz – Max-Planck-Institut)

visual relations through visual perception.[10]

The use of the framing device in art history goes all the way back to Giorgio Vasari (1511-1574) and his *Libro de' disegni* (Fig. 1). Starting out at the age of seventeen, Vasari compiled his collection in a scrapbook where he pasted drawings by various artists spanning the periods laid out in his *Lives of the Artists* (1550, 1568). It is no coincidence that Vasari elected to employ frames to build a convincing visual rhetoric. His project, after all, was contemporary with High Renaissance fresco cycles where the semiotics of the frame orchestrated effective rhetorical visual machines in the form of decorative systems – systems which the elite of the period conceived and were also able to decode. Dispersed across a number of repositories, the surviving leaves of Vasari's *Libro* tell us the following story: their creator used original drawings, which he combined in such a way that each leaf constitutes a complex critical and aesthetical argument. His approach is one of hermeneutics.[11]

A second, not so famous example, is that of Gustav Ludwig (1854-1905), who was a Carpaccio specialist. In 1904, after having mastered the technique of photography, he constructed a wooden model of the *Sant' Orsola* Church in Venice that would help him reconstitute the cycle of Carpaccio's paintings (Fig. 2).[12] He experimented with various placements and combinations of the narrative following the concordance of external and internal lightning conditions. When he was finally satisfied, he asked the photographer Tomaso Filippi to take pictures of the finished model and then retouched the photographs in order to create the context and thus provide a satisfactory rendering of his hypothesis. Apart from the fact that Ludwig's approach shows the enormous potential of the surrogate image as an agent of cognitive emancipation, it also provides an example of a model-frame where one could test a hypothesis of visual reconstruction. In his case we are closer to a heuristic process.

At this point one can hardly fail to mention Aby Warburg (1866-1929) and his *Mnemosyne Atlas*, with its imposing panels holding various visual documents such as artwork reproductions, newspaper clippings etc. (Fig. 3). Without wishing to add to the vast literature already dedicated to his oeuvre, it is worth noting that Warburg used the framing device not only in the already established form of the surrogate image; he also recorded his plates/montages, documenting thereby the stages of his argument. Moreover, he used frames as marks in order to design his argument before integrating it into his imposing panels.

Theoretical Observations

What theoretical observations can we make based on these examples? First of all, both Vasari and Ludwig mastered the *technique* that allowed them to build their projects and each invented his own way of "playing" with images in order to formulate complex visual paradigms/arguments.

In the first case Vasari used *disegno* – a practice placing the tracing of an idea conceived by the intellect in the center of the interpretative effort.[13] In the second instance, Ludwig found the tools and learned how to use them in order to give form not only to a final product – and this is where it becomes interesting – but to his own interpretative process. He built a wooden model, a miniature architectural "frame," in order to have the whole picture and to be able to test his hypotheses; the mockup allowed for performative actions[14] and enabled the recording of an interpretative effort. If the finalized albumen prints provide "contextualization," the photographs recording the intermediate stages of this project clearly testify to an approach stressing the messy, non-conclusive, ambiguous outcome.

One more parallel emerging from these examples is the question of the interface. Vasari built his own interface by drawing frames and adding ornamental figures that functioned as linking agents and deictic cues, thus influencing the perception of the drawings. Not only did he exploit the cognitive aspects of the frame as a device, but he also used its unifying qualities in order to assemble what one could call "a montage/ assemblage" of visual sources. The use of frames denotes a desire for appropriation. What Vasari created was a kind of hermeneutics playground.

Warburg took this approach much further. Recent scholarship has contributed essential observations concerning the "linking" aspect in Warburg's method;[15] the HyperImage[16] and Meta-Image[17] projects have been primarily based on these conclusions. I would like to bring into play a few more elements. Proceeding through a structural reading of his oeuvre, Maud Hagelstein has highlighted two instances. On the one hand we have the "framing operations" such as clippings and on the other the "montage effects," in other words a recombination of elements. One could say that the art historian destroyed the initial frame and imposed his own subjective frame[18] in order to work with his visual documents in the organic manner of finding and appreciating through a process which mutually fed the two poles.

In this dynamic process, the technical specificities of the medium, in this case the albumen prints, were exploited in combination with the dialectical properties of the framing device. Framing and assembling constitute the real epistemological richness of Warburg's Atlas,[19] where unexpected association of elements, flexibility of scale (the whole and the detail) were treated simultaneously and equally. But most importantly, Warburg built systems of representation, where the framing device operated as a structural element but also as node; its syntax alluded and enabled comparison, combination and recombination, close-looking, rearrangement and of course, linking. As part of a visual system though the images also brought into play their in-between space, the interval; a space where decisions are made, where pattern change begins to emerge. Stable frames and mobile frames, details and ensembles were thus combined in order to exploit the networking aspects of framing.

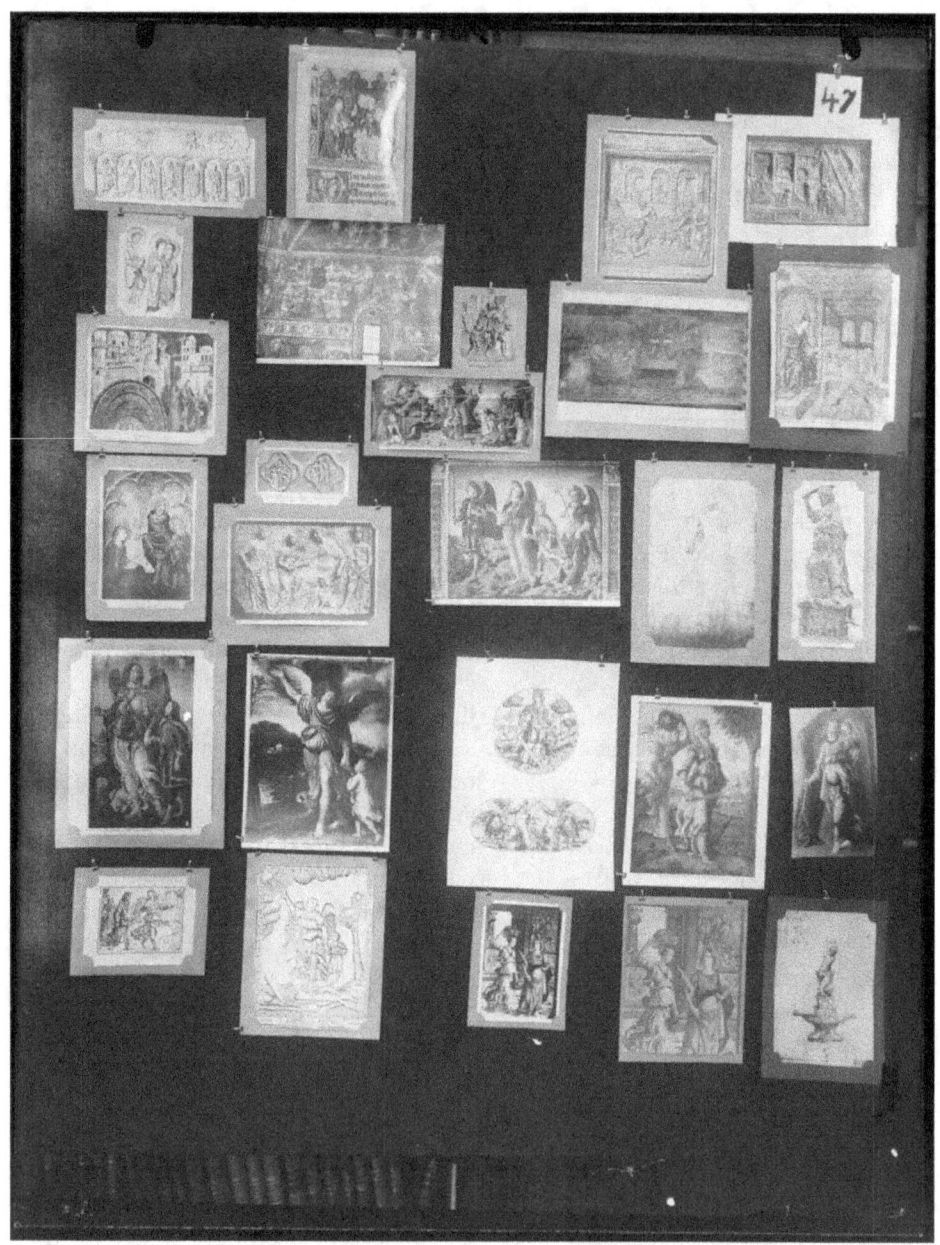

Figure 3: Aby Warburg, *Picture Atlas Mnemosyne*, 1928-29, Panel 47.
(Photo: © The Warburg Institute London)

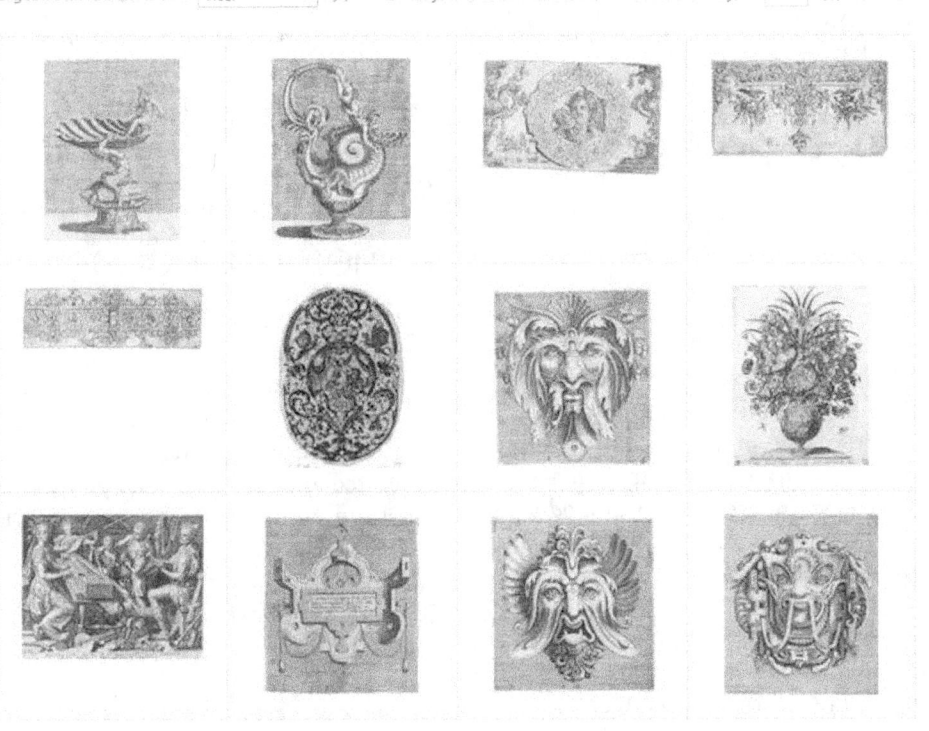

Figure 4: Results of the *Ornamental Prints* online catalog. Screenshot of website "Ornamental Prints Online" http://www.ornamentalprints.eu.
(© MAK – Austrian Museum of Applied Arts / Contemporary Art - UPM - Uměleckoprůmyslové museum Prague - Kunstbibliothek, Staatliche Museen zu Berlin – Preußischer Kulturbesitz)
Retrieval date: April 10, 2015

Panofsky was among the first to observe that Vasari's use of the framing device constituted a major turning point and in fact gave birth to art history.[20] Vasari created a structure that not only allowed for their aesthetic reception but also for their cognitive reception, thus encouraging a critical appropriation of the images.[21] Often referred to as the "first art historian," Vasari used *original* drawings and transformed them into objects of study by inscribing them within a frame whose style corresponded to his stylistic and aesthetic appreciation of the whole. His process of framing decontextualized the drawings from their initial context of creation and integrated them into his conception of art historical eras – they had been *repurposed*. His arguments can be refuted or criticized today but this has only become possible because of his process. Of course, with photography this repurposing dimension takes on its full potential, but it cannot be denied that as an archetypal figure for our discipline, Vasari's method proves the systemic nature of image appropriation and that of framing as its primary method, a need inherent in our *modus operandi*, which transcends the technical aspects of the medium across time.

One final note on the non-innocence of these systems. The examples discussed above do in fact carry the mark of their makers, their view of historical time, their conceptions of pattern evolution or style, the importance of context etc. Warburg for instance seems to have been influenced by Simmel's image of history, his "opening" of the frame and that of a transhistorical view.[22]

Art historical research protocols in the digital realm

Bearing in mind these theoretical observations and turning to the present, I would like to examine the use of the framing device in an array of digital environments. Following this I shall focus my attention on the potential of creating digital heuristic spaces which fully exploit the image-as-document.

Frames and framing: a method-inducing mechanism

If the frame is capable of shaping the reception of a given image within an interface, these qualities are not always exploited at their full capacity. In order to illustrate this argument let us briefly compare the Ornamental Prints Online (OPO) meta-catalog[23] with the Virtuelles Kupferstichkabinett (VK) catalog of the Herzog-Anton Ulrich Museum.[24]

Both projects present a collection of prints. The first one is a bit more specialized, pertaining solely to ornamental prints. What I wish to stress here is how the VK catalog alone proposes an "instrumented interface" and links the data in a way that makes sense for people who work with prints.

Figure 5: The *Virtuelles Kupferstichkabinett* results display. Multiple images have been selected; their frames are a lighter shade of grey.
(© Herzog-Anton Ulrich Museum, Braunschweig)

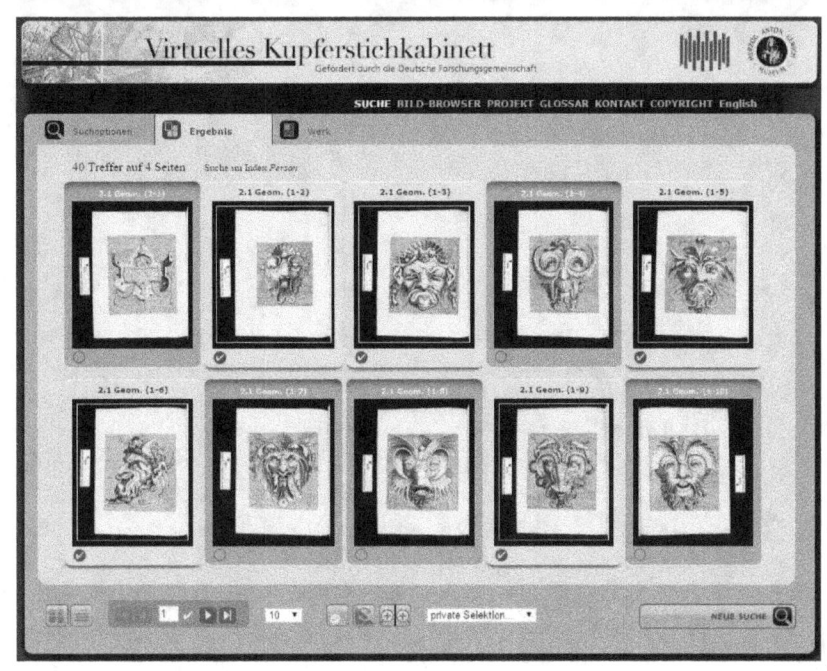

Figure 6: Results for "Adam and Eve" from the *Cranach Digital Archive*.
(© Cranach Digital Archive, 2015)

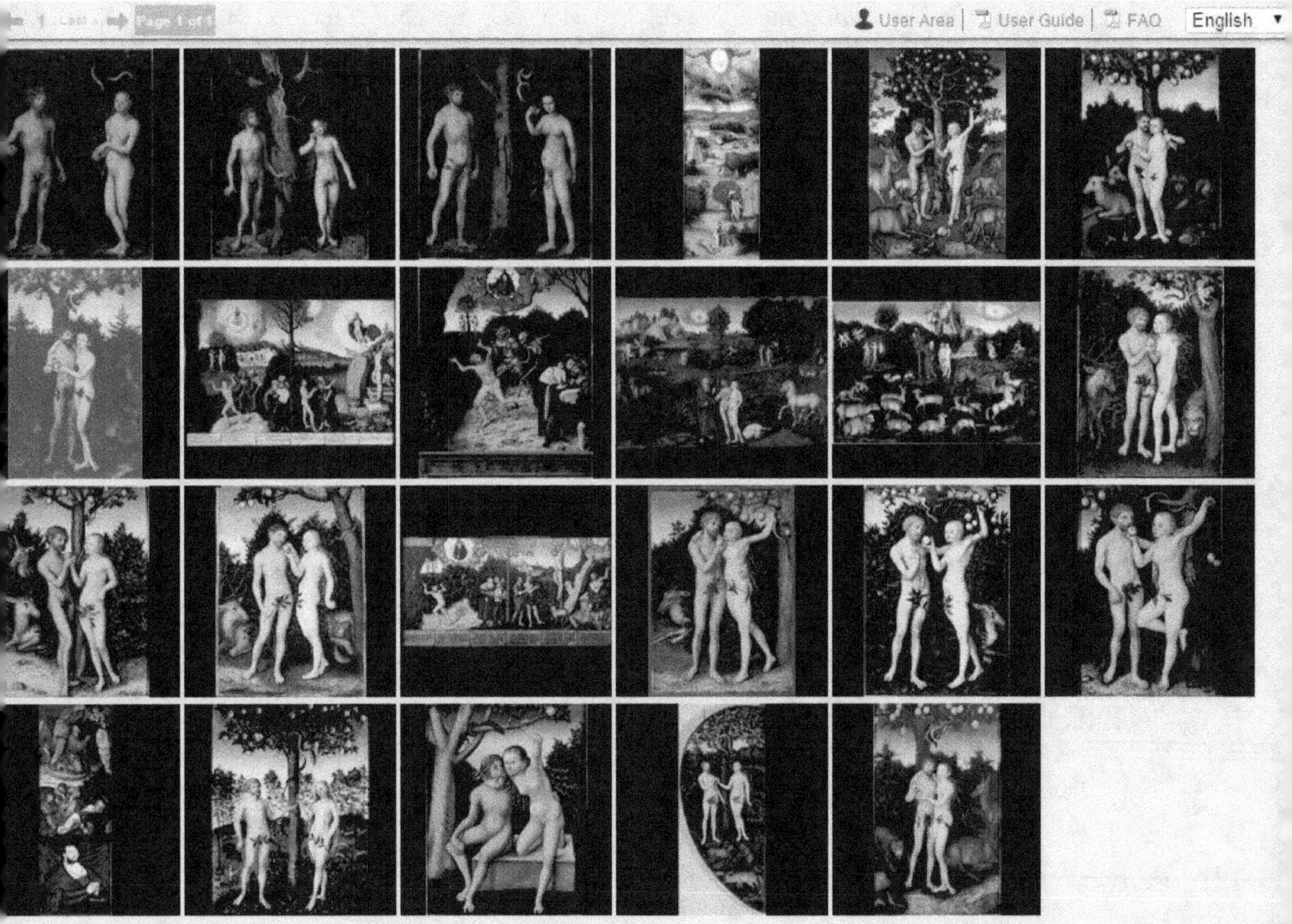

The fundamental difference of principle lies among other things in the theoretical foundations behind the use of frames. In the OPO catalog the frames simply present the image and they separate it from its surroundings (Fig. 4). By contrast, in the VK project the "slide frames" are not purely decorative (Fig. 5). By stressing the presence of the frames through visual means, these capture the user's attention and direct it towards the practice of a historically meaningful and deeply familiar process – that of spreading one's slides across a light-table in order to make a selection, by assembling and comparing multiple images. On the one hand we have an index destined for passive consultation comparable to a printed inventory – the *Illustrated Bartsch* for instance – while on the other the results page is only the beginning of the quest. By virtue of such features such as multiple selection, comparative zooming light tables and linking series of prints together the platform becomes not just a finding aid but a research resource adapted to its object of study, capable of becoming a *denkraum – a space for reflection*. Interestingly once the user enters the zooming light table workspace, the frame becomes invisible allowing one to concentrate solely on the object of study, in other words the print itself. It would seem that in this case the intensity of the framing device is calibrated according to the context of use.[25]

Towards systems of interpretation?

Ludwig's project, apart from alluding to projects of restitution of monuments no longer extant, sheds additional light on the potential of the surrogate image as document which in its digital form enables the researcher to use and visualize it in much more meaningful ways.

Turning to the Cranach Digital Archive, which is by all means an amazing project, we marvel at the high quality of the images and the fact that each of the artworks is presented as a unit of documentation along with a substantial critical apparatus (Fig. 6). In this case the interface functions as a documentation frame – but it is still not possible to actively engage with the image, in the way Ludwig did. There are many different versions of *Adam and Eve* for example, but one can only compare two images at a time and in addition to that the zooming levels are predefined. In other words the interface gets in the way of image manipulation.

If interface is an enunciation space where a subject is invoked,[26] then in this case this subject can only passively consume the information provided. One could of course propose that the ancestor of such a project is the traditional scholarly catalog. And yet the project has "selectively" integrated a feature stemming from a different tradition – that of the atlas. I am referring to the pre-visualization thumbnails view which reminds us of paradigms such as the plates of Seroux d'Agincourt's *L'histoire de l'art par ses monumens* [sic] (Fig. 7).[27] So, if in fact we have the possibility to mix and match scholarly precedents – and why shouldn't we? – why not create more dynamic creator-centered projects? Historically conscious instrumentation and critical apparatus play a crucial role

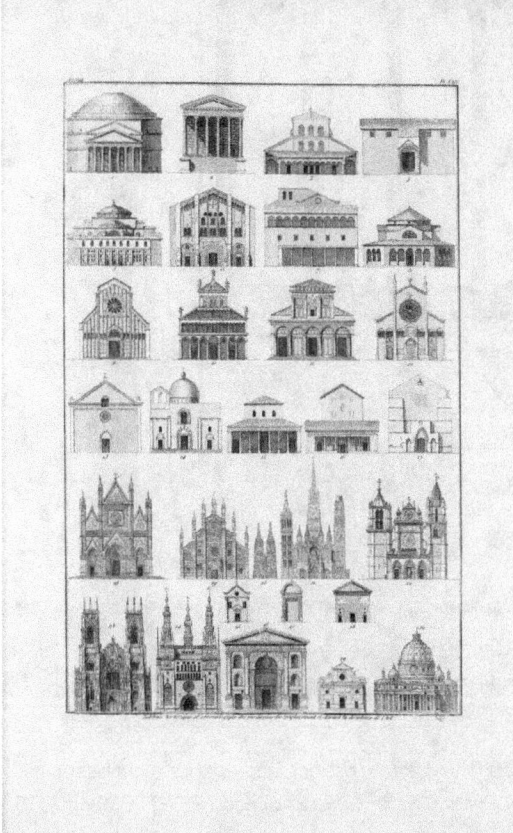

Figure 7 : *Tableau historique et chronologique des frontispices des temples, avant et durant la décadence de l'art*. Plate 64. Extract of : "Histoire de l'art par les monumens depuis sa décadence au IVe siècle jusqu'à son renouvellement au XIVe" / by J. B. L. G. Seroux d'Agincourt. Vol. IV. Paris: Treuttel and Würtz, 1823. Anonymous. Paris, bibliothèque de l'Institut National d'Histoire de l'Art, collections Jacques Doucet.
(Photo: © INHA, Dist. RMN-Grand Palais/image INHA)

here. Ludwig's example demonstrates how by thinking *through* a given interface one can create an instrument that goes beyond the optical metaphor of the Latin word *speculum* and gives way to an interpretative space.

The multiplication of frames and their mobility seem to be in the heart of more recent environments such as Mirador (Fig. 8) and the Virtual Mappa project (Fig. 9).[28] These two characteristics inevitably bring forward their impact on articulation and their potential for meaningful combination in the process of building a visually compelling argument.[29] How could we exploit the notion of "interval" in the digital environment?

Apart from being a device which presents, the frame is also a space in its own right and one that does not have to be necessarily transparent or invisible. What kind of instrumentation could a frame carry in order to allow for a meaningful appropriation/interpretation within a digital environment? Could this instrumentation differ from one frame to another within the same resource depending on the specificities of its content? Would it be desirable that a frame adapt to its content but also its context? Artworks are "anachronic" objects especially when it comes to interpreting them.[30] Could the instrumentation of the frame and its interaction with the rest of the system help us grasp that by playing on the separating/unifying dimension? By allowing their insertion into a completely different conception of time? By combining its different contexts (historical, art historical, critical evaluation, material history, history of collections, visual citations etc.) and materiality aspects? All these factors come with their individual "frames," which the interface could help either accentuate or keep more discreet depending on the type of question asked by the user.

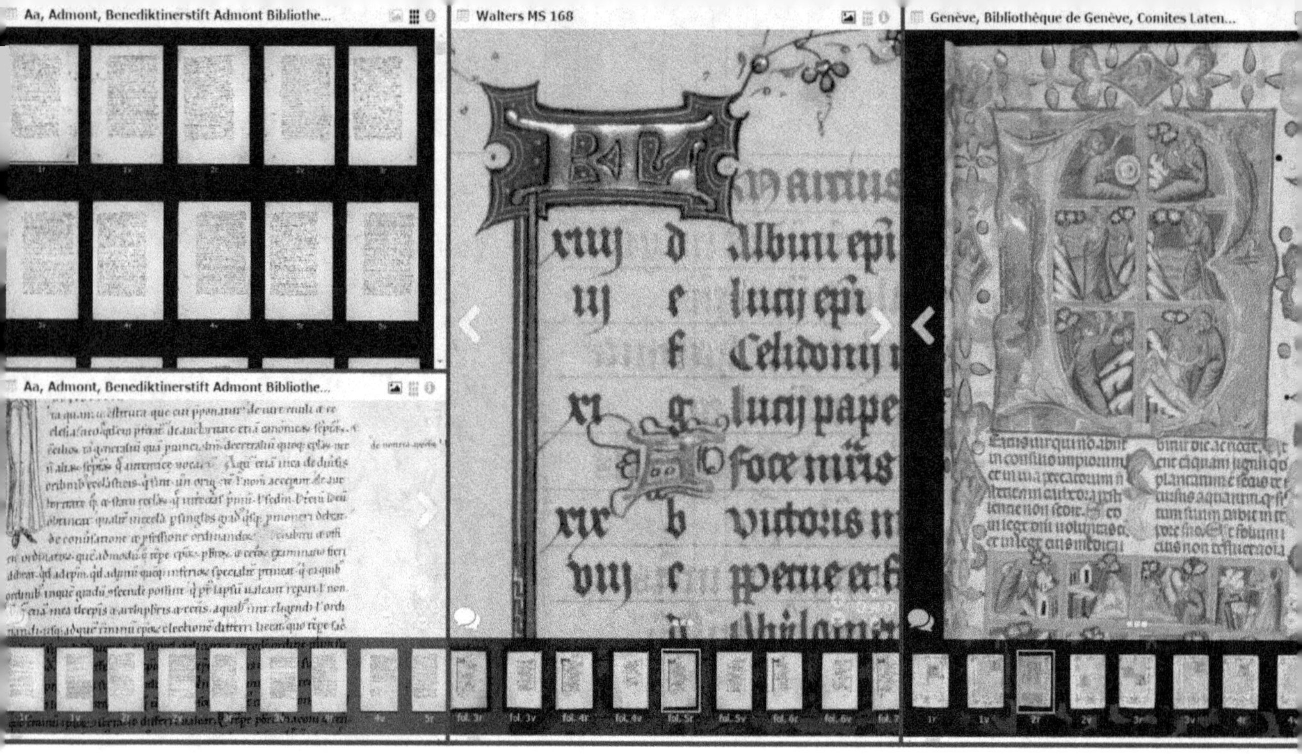

Figure 8: The *Mirador* project, screenshot of website.
http://projectmirador.org/demo/?json=552702fee4b06666571d23a1. Retrieval date: April 10, 2015

Figure 9: Screenshot of the *Virtual Mappa* project. Reproduced by permission of Martin K. Foys.

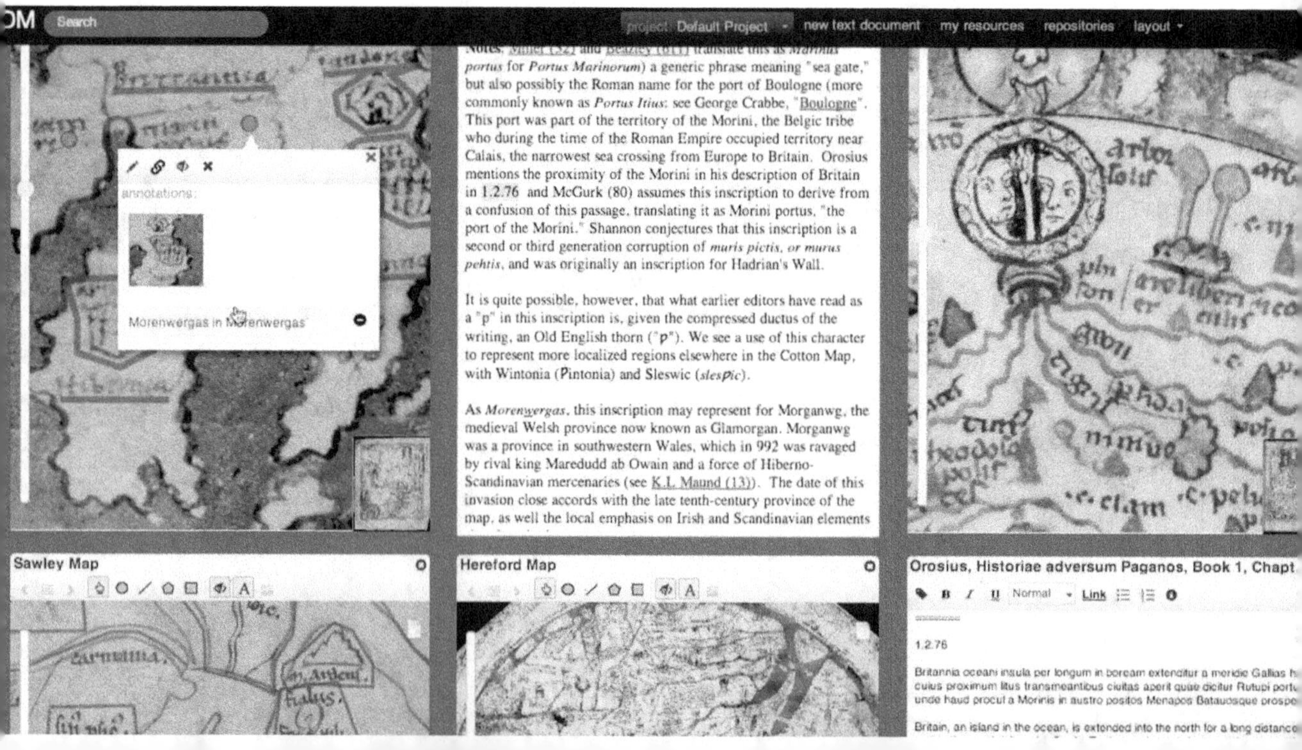

Imagine for instance comparing a fresco detail from Renaissance Rome with an illuminated manuscript border of the fourteenth century and an ancient Roman sarcophagus relief. You might not need the parallax view for the miniature, but you certainly need a 360° view of the sarcophagus and you need to see the detail of the fresco in context, perhaps also some preparatory drawings and relevant archival material. Going back to the miniature, you might want a thumbnails view of the entire book. Cropping, annotating and linking can follow and for their combination an additional space is required where a button, for instance, could allow for capturing and archiving of the workspace in its current phase. The full documentary value of these practices can emerge when the capacity to record and integrate in previous workflow are enabled.[31]

Conclusions

The objective of this essay is to underline the fundamental and constitutive dimension of image appropriation in the field of art history. In the enunciative system that is interface, the frame has a strategic role to play. It is capable of "decontextualizing" an artifact as well as reintegrating it into a new pattern of thought. As we have seen, the frame separates but also brings together; it provides an intermediate space where action and decision-making can occur. Viewed from the perspective of art historical methodologies I would argue that present environments should at least enable or accommodate previous methodologies.

Throughout the discussion I have chosen not to distinguish between reference resources and virtual research environments since my primary aim has been to shed light to the cognitive aspects of a common visual device and to stress its art historical prerogatives in the context of visual thinking. At this pivotal moment for digital art history it seems necessary to bear in mind the variety of methodologies in the field, the multiple angles and traditions from which we select to approach our objects of study. Even if the act of constructing an interpretative space carries seeds of interpretation itself, promoting for example a certain view of historical time, we could use this to our advantage by using frames to differentiate the dimensions of the object in relation to its various contexts. In other words, being flexible and intuitive is not merely an interface design issue; it touches the core of our practices.

Finally, it seems to me – and at this point I completely agree with Nuria Rodríguez Ortega's conclusions[32] – that this kind of specifically art historical epistemological awareness is essential if we want to bridge the gap between traditional methodologies and innovative computational practices. Historically relevant epistemological perspectives are just as important as the vision of things that we could not do before. One way to bring this kind of discourse into play is by integrating it into our peer-reviewing protocols and by training students not only learning how to use new software and resources[33] but to critically process these resources and situate them within a methodological framework, thus building a continuity with the previous phases of the field, a continuity that could only reinforce the meaningful use of resources in the future as well as the questions asked. Apart from finding the tool which best serves our needs, we should also be conscious of *how* we want to *see* our object of study, now and in the future.

Notes

[1] Anne Collins Goodyear and Paul B. Jaskot, "Digital Art History Takes Off," *CAA News / College Art Association*, October 7 2014, accessed January 22, 2015, http://www.collegeart.org/news/2014/10/07/digital-art-history-takes-off/. A substantial body of literature is already available. See for example, Corinne Welger-Barboza, "L'histoire de l'art et sa technologie - Concordance des Temps," *L'Observatoire Critique*, December 4, 2012, accessed January 30, 2015, http://observatoire-critique.hypotheses.org/1862; Murtha Baca, Susan Edwards, and Francesca Albrezzi, "Rethinking Art History," *The Getty Iris*, March 4, 2013, accessed January 30, 2015, http://blogs.getty.edu/iris/getty-voices-rethinking-art-history/; Murtha Baca and Anne Helmreich, "Introduction," *Visual Resources* 29, no. 1–2 (2013): 1–4, accessed January 23, 2015, doi: 10.1080/01973762.2013.761105; Johanna Drucker, "Is There a 'Digital' Art History?" *Visual Resources* 29, no. 1–2 (2013): 5–13, accessed January 30, 2015, doi: 10.1080/01973762. 2013.761106; Nuria Rodríguez Ortega, "Digital Art History: An Examination of Conscience," *Visual Resources* 29, no. 1–2 (2013): 129–33, accessed January 30, 2015, doi: 10.1080/01973762.2013. 761124; Hubertus Kohle, *Digitale Bildwissenschaft* (Glückstadt: Hülsbusch, 2013), accessed January 30, 2015, http://archiv.ub.uni-heidelberg.de/artdok/2185/; Diane Zorich, *Transitioning to a Digital World: Art History, Its Research Centers, and Digital Scholarship*. Report to the Samuel H. Kress Foundation and the Roy Rosenzweig Center for History and New Media. George Mason University, May 2012, accessed January 03, 2015, http://www.kressfoundation.org/research/transitioning_to_a_digital_world/

[2] Erwin Panofsky, "Art History as a Humanistic Discipline," in *The Meaning of the Humanities*, ed. Theodore M. Greene (Princeton, NJ: Princeton University Press, 1940), 106-107.

[3] Johanna Drucker, "Graphesis: Visual Knowledge Production and Representation," *paj:The Journal of the Initiative for Digital Humanities, Media, and Culture* 2, no 1 (2010): 3, accessed January 23, 2015, https://journals.tdl.org/paj/index.php/paj/article/view/4.

[4] Johanna Drucker, *Graphesis: Visual Forms of Knowledge Production*, metaLAB Projects (Cambridge, MA: Harvard University Press, 2014).

[5] An earlier version of this essay was presented during the 102nd annual conference of the College Art Association in February 2014. I would like to thank Victoria Scott, Martine Denoyelle, Anne Helmreich, Max Marmor and Emmanuel Chateau for reading drafts and for providing me with much useful feedback.

[6] Drucker, "Is There a 'Digital' Art History?"; Rodríguez Ortega, "Digital Art History"; Zorich, *Transitioning to a Digital World*.

[7] Surrogate images reproducing decorative cycles of the Renaissance testify to the neglect of the syntactic dimension by omitting the margins, where their syntax and logic resides. More recently art historical research has begun to take into account decorative systems and study their syntax and modes of enunciation. In this context the frame holds a dominant position as a mediator between the decorated space and the viewer. The theoretical underpinnings of these studies are primarily based on the work of Louis Marin.

[8] Groupe μ, *Traité du signe visuel. Pour une rhétorique de l'image* (Paris: Seuil, 1992), 378.

[9] Louis Marin, "Le cadre de la représentation et quelques-unes de ses figures," *Cahiers du Musée national d'art moderne*, no. 24 (1988): 63–81; Marin, "Figures de la réception dans la représentation moderne de peinture," in *De la représentation*, ed. Daniel Arasse et al. (Paris: Seuil/Gallimard, 1994), 313–28.

[10] For a thorough analysis on the role of the framing device in humanist practices, see Drucker, *Graphesis*, 2014, esp. 138–179.

[11] Stefania Caliandro, "Introduction au métavisuel: le *Libro de' disegni* de Giorgio Vasari," in *Images d'images. Le métavisuel dans l'art visuel* (Paris: L'Harmattan, 2008), 15–35.

[12] Costanza Caraffa, "From Photo Libraries to Photo Archives: On the Epistemolons," in *Photo Archives and the Photographic Memory of Art History*, ed. Costanza Caraffa, (Berlin/Munich: Deutscher Kunstverlag, 2011), 11–44. For the complete image set see the online exhibition *Gus-*

tav Ludwig. *The Photographic Bequest* of the KHI in Florence, at http://photothek.khi.fi.it/documents/oau/00000045.

[13] See Anne Burdick and Johanna Drucker, *Digital_humanities* (Cambridge, MA: MIT Press, 2012). Interestingly what is placed in the heart of this book project is design.

[14] For further discussion on the aspects of performative engagement, see Johanna Drucker, "Performative Materiality and Theoretical Approaches to Interface." 7, no. 1 (2013), accessed January 30, 2015, http://www.digitalhumanities.org/dhq/vol/7/1/000143/000143.html.

[15] For example, see Lisa Dieckmann, Anita Kliemann, and Martin Warnke, "Meta-Image – Forschungsumgebung Für Den Bilddiskurs in Der Kunstgeschichte," *CMS Journal*, no. 35 (2012), accessed January 23, 2015, http://edoc.hu-berlin.de/cmsj/35/dieckmann-lisa-11/XML/diekmann-11.xml.; Warnke and Dieckmann, "Prometheus meets Meta-Image: implementations of Aby Warburg's methodical approach in the digital era," *Visual Studies* (forthcoming).

[16] *HyperImage*, at http://hyperimage.ws/en/.

[17] *Meta-Image*, at http://www2.leuphana.de/meta-image/index.php; for additional bibliography, see http://www2.leuphana.de/meta-image/Publikationen.php

[18] Maud Hagelstein, "L'histoire des images selon Warburg: Mnémosyne et ses opérations de cadrage," in *Cadre, Seuil, Limite. La question de la frontière dans la théorie de l'art* (Brussels: La lettre volée, 2010), 257.

[19] Ibid., 258.

[20] Erwin Panofsky, "Le feuillet initial du '*Libro*' de Vasari," in *L'oeuvre d'art et ses significations. Essais sur les arts "visuels,"* tr. Marthe et Bernard Teyssèdre (1969; repr., Paris: Gallimard, 2004), 138, 186.

[21] Caliandro, "De l'usage d'images par la critique", in *Images d'images*, 10. "Pourtant, il est fortement remarquable que l'idée de créer une structure de réception visuelle aie déjà été conçue à l'époque moderne et par le même auteur censé avoir posé les fondements de l'histoire de l'art occidental".

[22] Hagelstein, "L'histoire des images selon Warburg," 271.

[23] *Ornamental Prints Online*, at http://www.ornamentalprints.eu/. Some days before the publication of this article the author observed that the website is no longer available online. The prints can now be consulted through the separate collections of each partner institution.

[24] *Virtuelles* Kupferstichkabinett, at http://www.virtuelles-kupferstichkabinett.de/.

[25] For a detailed commentary of this resource, see Elli Doulkaridou, "Vers les cabinets d'estampes en ligne: Le cas du Virtuelles Kupferstichkabinett," *L'observatoire Critique*, January 9, 2011, accessed January 30, 2015, http://observatoire-critique.hypotheses.org/775.

[26] Drucker, "Performative Materiality," para. 33.

[27] J.B.L.G. Seroux d'Agincourt, *L'histoire de l'art par ses monumens depuis sa décadence au IVe siècle jusqu'à son renouvellement au XIVe*, 6 vols. (Paris: Treuttel et Wurtz, 1823). Now also available online, http://www.purl.org/yoolib/inha/8909 to 8914. See also Welger-Barboza, "L'histoire de l'art et sa technologie."

[28] *Mirador* is an open access platform which allows the user to display documents from various collections across the web, at http://projectmirador.org; *Virtual Mappa* is part of the DM project. For more information and other implementations, see http://schoenberginstitute.org/dm-tools-for-digital-annotation-and-linking/; other good examples are *Manuscriptorium*, at http://www.manuscriptorium.com/ and the *Chinese Painting and Calligraphy* catalog of the Seattle Museum of art, at http://chinesepainting.seattleartmuseum.org/. Belonging to the OSCI initiative the latter presents an interesting use of sliders combined with adapted static and mobile contents.

[29] Warburg's models still linger and the *Meta-Image* project definitely steers in that direction. The *Getty Scholars' Workspace* could equally provide some answers in the near future, see http://www.getty.edu/research/scholars/research_projects/

[30] Georges Didi-Huberman, *Devant le temps: histoire de l'art et anachronisme des images* (Paris: les Éditions de Minuit, 2000).

[31] Tiziana Serena, "The Words of the Photo Archive," in Caraffa, *Photo Archives*, 57.

[32] Rodríguez Ortega, "Digital Art History," esp. 132–133.

[33] Matthew P. Long and Roger C. Schonfeld, *Supporting the Changing Practices of Art Historians* (Ithaka S+R, April 30, 2014), 47, accessed April 30, 2014, http://www.sr.ithaka.org/sites/default/files/reports/SR_Support-Changing-Research-ArtHist_20140429.pdf.

Bibliography

Baca, Murtha, Susan Edwards, and Francesca Albrezzi. "Rethinking Art History." *The Getty Iris*, March 4, 2013. Accessed January 30, 2015. http://blogs.getty.edu/iris/getty-voices-rethinking-art-history/.

Baca, Murtha, and Anne Helmreich. "Introduction." *Visual Resources* 29, no. 1–2 (2013): 1–4. Accessed January 30, 2015. doi:10.1080/01973762.2013.761105.

Burdick, Anne, and Johanna Drucker. *Digital_humanities*. Cambridge, MA: MIT Press, 2012.

Caliandro, Stefania. *Images d'images. Le métavisuel dans l'art visuel*. Paris: L'Harmattan, 2008.

———. "De l'usage d'images par la critique : Warburg et les détours du visuel." In *Images d'images. Le métavisuel dans l'art visuel*, 95–127. Paris: L'Harmattan, 2008.

———. "Introduction au métavisuel : Le *Libro de' Disegni* de Giorgio Vasari." In *Images d'images. Le métavisuel dans l'art visuel*, 15–35. Paris: L'Harmattan, 2008.

Caraffa, Costanza. *Photo Archives and the Photographic Memory of Art History*, edited by Costanza Caraffa. Berlin/Munich: Deutscher Kunstverlag, 2011.

———. "From Photo Libraries to Photo Archives: On the Epistemological Potential of Art-Historical Photo Collections." In *Photo Archives and the Photographic Memory of Art History*, edited by Costanza Caraffa, 11–44. Berlin/Munich: Deutscher Kunstverlag, 2011.

Collins Goodyear, Anne, and Paul B. Jaskot. "Digital Art History Takes Off." *CAA News, College Art Association*, October 7, 2014. Accessed January 22, 2015. http://www.collegeart.org/news/2014/10/07/digital-art-history-takes-off/.

Didi-Huberman, Georges. *Devant le temps: histoire de l'art et anachronisme des images*, Paris: Les Éditions de minuit, 2000.

Dieckmann, Lisa, Anita Kliemann, and Martin Warnke. "Meta-Image – Forschungsumgebung für den Bilddiskurs in der Kunstgeschichte." *CMS Journal*, no. 35 (2012). Accessed January 30, 2015. http://edoc.hu-berlin.de/cmsj/35/dieckmann-lisa-11/XML/diekmann-11.xml.

Doulkaridou, Elli. "Vers les cabinets d'estampes en ligne : Le cas du Virtuelles Kupferstichkabinett." *L'observatoire critique*, January 9, 2011. Accessed January 30, 2015. http://observatoire-critique.hypotheses.org/775.

Drucker, Johanna. "Graphesis: Visual Knowledge Production and Representation." *paj: The Journal of the Initiative for Digital Humanities, Media, and Culture* 2, no. 1 (2010). Accessed January 30, 2015. https://journals.tdl.org/paj/index.php/paj/article/view/4.

———. *Graphesis: Visual Forms of Knowledge Production*. MetaLABprojects. Cambridge, MA: Harvard University Press, 2014.

———. "Is There a 'Digital' Art History?" *Visual Resources* 29, no. 1–2 (2013): 5–13. Accessed January 30, 2015. doi:10.1080/01973762.2013.761106.

———. "Performative Materiality and Theoretical Approaches to Interface." 7, no. 1 (2013). Accessed January 30, 2015. http://www.digitalhumanities.org/dhq/vol/7/1/000143/000143.html.

Groupe μ. *Traité du signe visuel. Pour une rhétorique de l'image*. Paris: Seuil, 1992.

Hagelstein, Maud. "L'histoire des images selon Warburg : Mnémosyne et ses opérations de cadrage." In *Cadre, seuil, limite. La question de la frontière dans la théorie de l'art*, edited by Thierry Lenain and Rudy Steinmetz, 251–79. Brussels: La lettre volée, 2010.

Kohle, Hubertus. *Digitale Bildwissenschaft*. Glückstadt: Hülsbusch, 2013. Accessed January 30, 2015. http://archiv.ub.uni-heidelberg.de/artdok/2185/.

Long, Matthew P., and Roger C. Schonfeld. *Supporting the Changing Practices of Art Historians*. Ithaka S+R, April 30, 2014. Accessed April 30, 2014. http://www.sr.ithaka.org/sites/default/files/reports/SR_Support-Changing-Research-ArtHist_20140429.pdf.

Marin, Louis. "Figures de la réception dans la représentation moderne de peinture." In *De la représentation*, edited by Daniel Arasse, Alain Cantillon, Giovanni Careri, Danièle Cohn, Pierre-Antoine Fabre and Françoise Marin, 313–28. Paris: Seuil/Gallimard, 1994.

———. "Le cadre de la représentation et quelques-unes de ses figures." *Cahiers du Musée national d'art moderne*, no. 24 (1988): 63–81.

Panofsky, Erwin. "Art History as a Humanistic Discipline." In *The Meaning of the Humanities*, edited by Theodore M. Greene, 89-118. Princeton, NJ: Princeton University Press, 1940.

———. "Le feuillet initial du '*Libro*' de Vasari." In *L'œuvre d'art et ses significations. Essais sur les arts "visuels,"* translated by Marthe et Bernard Teyssèdre, 137-87, 1969. Reprint, Paris: Gallimard, 2004.

Rodríguez Ortega, Nuria. "Digital Art History: An Examination of Conscience." *Visual Resources* 29, no. 1-2 (2013): 129-33. Accessed January 30, 2015. doi:10.1080/01973762.2013.761124.

Serena, Tiziana. "The Words of the Photo Archive." In *Photo Archives and the Photographic Memory of Art History*, edited by Costanza Caraffa, 57-71. Berlin/München: Deutscher Kunstverlag, 2011.

Warnke, Martin and Lisa Dieckmann, "Prometheus meets Meta-Image: implementations of Aby Warburg's methodical approach in the digital era," *Visual Studies*, forthcoming.

Welger-Barboza, Corinne. "L'histoire de l'art et sa technologie - Concordance des temps." *L'observatoire Critique*, December 4, 2012. Accessed January 30, 2015. http://observatoire-critique.hypotheses.org/1862.

Zorich, Diane. *Transitioning to a Digital World: Art History, Its Research Centers, and Digital Scholarship*. Report to the Samuel H. Kress Foundation and the Roy Rosenzweig Center for History and New Media. George Mason University, May 2012. Accessed January 03, 2015. http://www.kressfoundation.org/research/transitioning_to_a_digital_world/.

Elli Doulkaridou is a PhD candidate in art history at Centre d'histoire de l'art de la Renaissance, University of Paris I Panthéon-Sobonne. Between 2011 and 2014 she was also a research assistant at the Institut national d'histoire de l'art. Her research, under the supervision of Professor Philippe Morel, concerns Roman illuminated manuscripts of the first half of the 16th century. Part of her thesis will be focusing on digital practices and methodological shifts in the domain of illuminated manuscripts. Between 2009 and 2011, she taught the course "Management of digital resources" in the department of art history at her university. She has also led workshops on digital art history for two summers at the European Summer University in Digital Humanities (University of Leipzig).

Correspondence e-mail: elli.dou@gmail.com

Interview

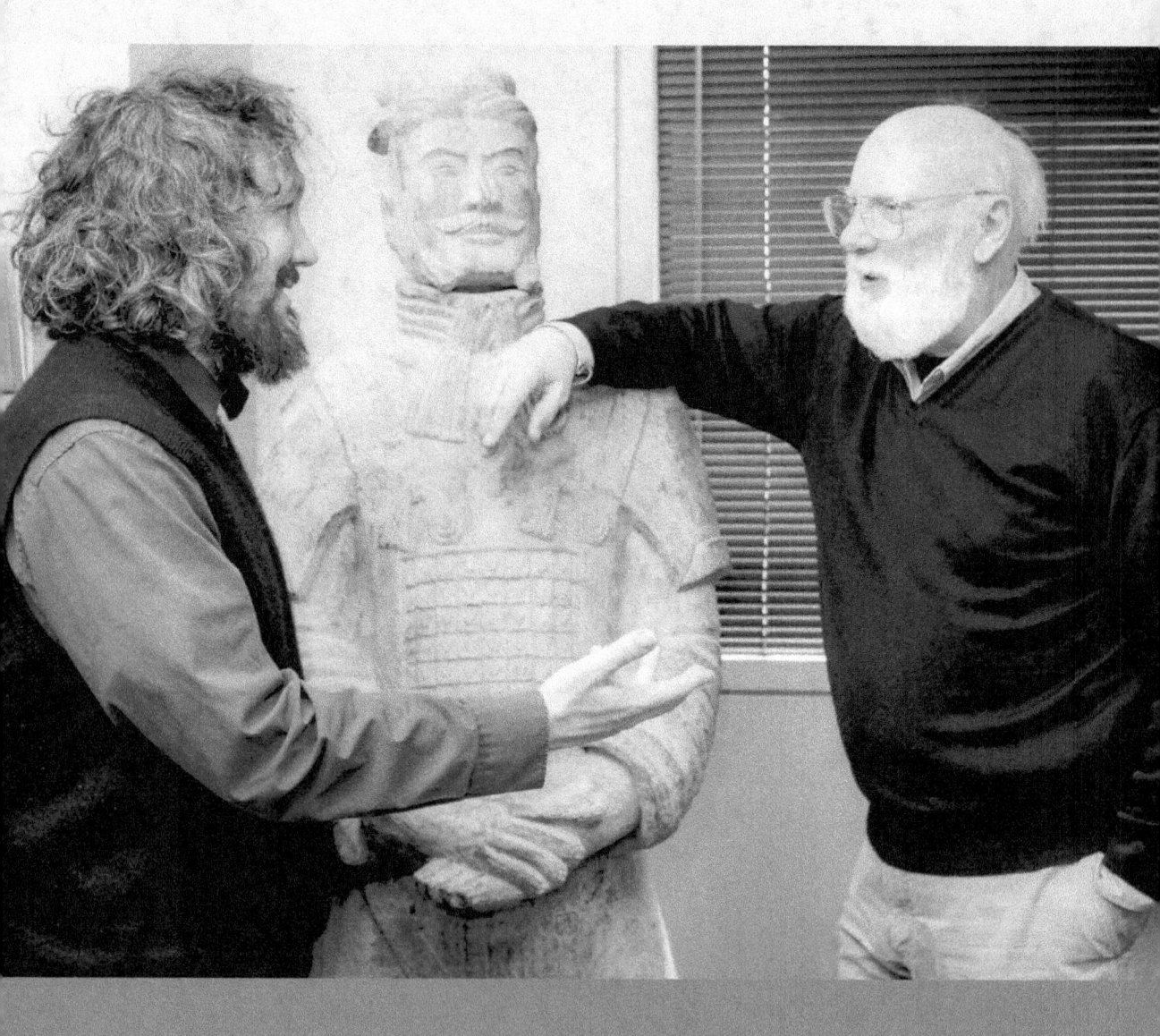

Invited Article

On Applying Signal Processing to Computational Art History: an Interview

Park Doing and C. Richard Johnson, Jr.

*P*ark and Rick sit across a desk facing each other in Rick's office in Cornell's Engineering College. We see Park's back and Rick's face. They are dressed in winter clothes. Overseeing the proceedings, peering over Rick's shoulder at Park, is a six foot tall Terra Cotta Warrior that has made the journey from China.

The view is into Rick's office with a small window in the back wall offering a view of barren tree limbs and falling snow. Rick's office is situated between closed doors to offices on the same hall. The office on the left houses a professor expert in information theory. On the right a professor specializing in medical image processing.

Along the left wall in Rick's office stands a bookcase with treatises, dissertations, books, and volumes about control systems and signal processing and art history and conservation. The top of the bookshelves displays pictures of Rick's graduate students. Among the awards advertised on the wall above the bookcase is Rick's prized Eagle Scout certificate. The warrior is in the back left corner of the office.

Along the right wall of the office hang three full-size prints of Van Gogh's "Bedroom": color, false-color infrared, and raking light.

Park has been observing Rick for years, with Rick luring him along. Everyone, including Rick, knows Park has written about 'cultural' battles between physicists and biologists (not to mention technicians and administrators) in a particle physics laboratory, and about interactions between experts and 'lay persons' with regard to issues of science and public welfare. Rick had previously explained to Park how he was entering the world of art history, museums, curators, and conservators, and how much he was learning in the process about approaches (some successful) to cross-disciplinary research. Imagining the potential for insights from an expert observer, Rick offered Park access to a front row seat for viewing a real-time attempt at cross-cultural collaboration between technologists (represented by signal processors) and humanists (represented by art historians and conservators). Park couldn't possibly say no to such an offer. We are about to observe one of their bull sessions.

Park looks down from the Terra Cotta soldier's eyes to Rick's.

RJ – OK – how do you want to get started?

PD – I sent you that list of questions. We could go through them.

Park Doing (left) and Rick Johnson with the Chinese Warrior in Rick's office.
(Photo: Jessica E. S. Edmister, ECE, Cornell University)

Rick turns away from Park toward his computer monitor.

RJ – Sure. Sure. OK. Let me get that email.

Park interrupts this gesture.

PD – First though, let me just step back and ask you a big picture question.

Rick answers, still looking sideways.

RJ – OK. What's the question?

PD – Why did you get into the application of signal processing to problems in art history? What is interesting about it to you?

Pause, Rick still looking at screen rather than at Park.

RJ – What is interesting about it to you?

Park is not flustered by this push back. Both Park and Rick exhibit nothing but comfort with the flow evidently familiar from many previous such episodes of wandering banter.

PD – Well… I have to think a little… for me it comes down to a scene in Gabriel Garcia Marquez's 100 Years of Solitude. Toward the end of the novel, the story is told of a priest and a peasant playing chess beneath a tree, but the game can never end because each of them is playing with a different set of rules. I'm forever intrigued by that kind of situation.

Rick laughs.

RJ – That's the question? It's exactly your type of question. When there's no blueprint for picking the problems – how do you pick the problems?! This is especially critical in trying to bring two areas together that are deemed by all to have little to no overlap. In all of my research subjects, there are two languages to learn, one for the area of the exploited technical expertise and another for the domain of the subject to which it is to be applied. It has always been that way for me.

My first crossover between control systems and digital signal processing (DSP) began during my PhD studies in the 1970s when the researchers in these two subjects occupied two distinct worlds, with separate journals, separate conferences, etc… This is difficult to visualize now as the two fields are intertwined in many ways with a large number of top researchers active in both communities. Back then, I saw issues in adaptive filtering popular among the DSP crowd that were being addressed in slightly different versions in recursive system identification research in the control systems community. I was one of a small group – at first – of researchers exploiting and explaining this interconnection. That worked out well.

PD – So even within engineering – those were two different worlds.

Scientists face language and cultural barriers.

Park's tone conveys that he is trying to push Rick to acknowledge the disunity in science and engineering, the bricolage of what appears from the outside to be monolithic endeavor unified by shared understandings – that scientists themselves face language and cultural barriers.

RJ – Absolutely. At the time.

PD – So, you've already done this crossover-thing before.

RJ – Well, Yes and no. This time is much more extreme in the differences encountered. The institutions – universities and museums in the US and Europe – are different. Their languages are different. Research conventions are different. Different worldviews. A lot to overcome in getting us on the same page.

PD – Let's talk about worldviews. I would say that you have a 'signal processing worldview'. You see the world in signals. You see the elements of those signals and how they can be broken down, rearranged, reformulated even.

RJ – I agree. Continuing that train of thought, the art expert's reliance on examination of images viewed as signals suggests that signal processing can somehow assist art investigation. Actually, that line of thinking gave me the confidence to seek out ways to enter the museum world to observe the users of technology within the museum, i.e. the conservators, in the hope of seeing where my expertise could be applied. My PhD minor in art history helped me speak at a basic level in their language. I was keenly aware from the start that I could not resort to mathematical language or thinking in describing to them what types of problems I could tackle.

PD – In addition to the cross-cultural challenges, I've heard you remark on the unexpectedly large amount of time required to obtain access to sufficiently-high-resolution digitized images of art works.

RJ – The time commitment to gain access to scientific quality data has proven formidable. It remains a high barrier for new entrants into this growing field from outside the museum community. Fortunately, this is beginning to change.

"Without data no theoretical problem can be posed that will have practical impact."

You run into this in pure engineering too – in the middle phase of my career we were working on receivers for terrestrial broadcast high definition television before it existed on a wide scale. For competitive reasons, companies with field data were reluctant to share it with perceived competitors. And without data it is nearly impossible to pose an academically appealing theoretical problem that will have practical impact. The downside of working with real data is that it comes with all the nasties in it that complicate the specific problem's solution. But, having the data lets you raise questions that you do not know to raise without the data. That's the whole point. Real data helps you ask the right questions, and get useful answers.

PD – Why do you think painting data was made available to you?

RJ – Basically, I was very lucky with my first museum contact: the Van Gogh Museum in Amsterdam. In 2006, when I had my first meeting with their research and conservation management, they agreed right away to grant me the access to observe their conservators in action in my hunt for promising issues for collaboration. In exchange I offered to organize an international workshop the museum would host that would bring image processing experts to talk – without using mathematics – to art experts about computer-based tools for brushwork style classification.

Eighteen months later, we had identified the thread counting problem. The Van Gogh Museum ultimately provided us scans of x-radiographs of all of their paintings on canvas by van Gogh. They also approached other museums with requests for scans of their x-radiographs of van Gogh paintings on canvas. I learned that museums are used to sharing data with other museums, but not with outsiders like me. The museums have something to offer each other, i.e. access to images of artworks in each other's collections. At first, I had nothing to offer.

PD – What other attitudes/procedures did you have to adapt to?

RJ – I promised not to ask for the three things I knew they did not have to offer: money, space, or staff time.

PD – Tell me more about getting started on thread counting and weave matching?

RJ – In the beginning, I went to the Van Gogh Museum for a 10-day visit every 3 months or so. One day they said we were going to count threads. I asked to see a document beforehand that tells about this procedure and got blank looks. The concept of standard procedures, i.e. detailed algorithms for capturing measured data in a standard way, was itself not standard to them. When they showed me the x-radiograph images and taught me to count the threads visible under magnification, I recognized this task as a measurement of period that could be done on a scale unimaginable manually with the use of a Fourier transform. I would be helping to answer a question they wanted to answer.

PD – And weave matching came out of that?

> "We started with the goal of automating thread counting."

RJ – Well, yes. But nobody said, "We're going to invent a weave map." We started with the goal of automating thread counting. With that you can count not just the threads in a few sections of the painting, but in every section of the painting – and in every painting. So, after I got my first basic Fourier analysis program to work, I said to the Van Gogh Museum people that we could count all the paintings in their museum. They laughed. We started with x-radiographs for about 30 paintings. I realized later that they thought I was a funny guy – so American, wants to rush and do everything. I resolved to hew more to what I saw as the Dutch style of consensus decision-making where individuals are expected to suppress public display of their personal ambitions.

PD – So, a cultural difference beyond art and science?

RJ – Yes.

PD – Please continue.

The color-coded maps of local computations of weave density (threads/cm) reveal a matching stripe pattern in a pair of paintings by Vermeer.
(Image: Don H. Johnson, ECE, Rice University)
[For further details see W. Liedtke, C. R. Johnson, Jr., and D. H. Johnson, "Canvas Matches in Vermeer: A Case Study in the Computer Analysis of Fabric Supports," Metropolitan Museum Journal, vol. 47 (2012): 99-106.]

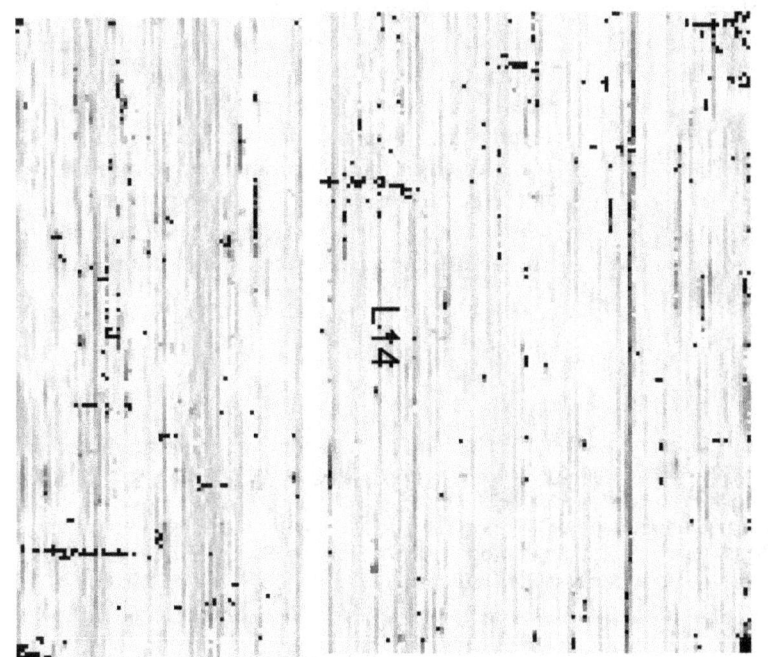

"We saw this pattern as a fingerprint for canvas from the same roll."

RJ – Weave maps emerged as we considered ways to present our count data. I knew a table with numbers was just about the worst thing we could do. That would go against what I was learning about how to communicate with art experts. It needed to be visual. I was working with people in the art community who are sublimely visually adept. If we could get it right, they would see it in a second. We color-coded the weave densities that were automatically counted and presented them as they covered the canvas. When we saw the vertical bands of color emerging we saw this pattern as a fingerprint for canvas from the same roll. You could see it clearly. I remember when I first presented an image of a match at a conference for conservators. I unveiled it and there was an audible gasp in the room. They got it right away. The weave map is now accepted as a new object with which to ask and answer questions about paintings on canvas.

PD – After the canvas studies and weave matching, the photo paper analysis came about. How did that start?

RJ – For two months in 2010 I spent half of each week visiting the Museum of Modern Art looking for a task suited to the application of image processing. I met with their conservation scientists and paper conservators. I learned that photo paper is made for its texture and could be classified by observing the changes in reflectance as the paper sample was moved around under a bright light. Raking light is a standard illumination for revealing modest surface texture variations by their shadow pattern. We chose to collect raking light images of photographic paper at a microscopic scale. It took me over a year and a half to convince the paper experts that we needed images of some sets of paper for which the classification is known to allow us to build algorithms. While museums are most curious regarding the objects about which their knowledge is uncertain or simply lacking – to start we need images known to be a match. We need them in order to be able to design and test the accuracy of our candidate algorithms. Once we built such a dataset suitable for algorithm development and testing, the groups pursuing different textural strategies for classification were all able to show promise in using raking light images of historic photographic paper as a proxy for classification by metadata, i.e. manufacturer, surface finish, brand, pe-

> *"That encourages the pursuit of automating photographic paper classification."*

Raking light images of 1.00 x 1.35 cm patches from two different 20th century black and white photographic papers displaying their distinct textures. (Photo: P. Messier, Messier Reference Collection)
[For further details see C. R. Johnson, Jr. and others, "Pursuing Automated Classification of Historic Photographic Papers from Raking Light Images," Journal of the American Institute for Conservation, Vol. 53, No. 3 (2014): 159-170.]

riod of manufacture. Just last year we published a paper in the art conservation literature on this study that encourages the pursuit of automating photographic paper classification.

PD – And what about the chain line work?

RJ – That came about a little differently, since I had already done some useful work with the weave mapping and photographic paper, I didn't have to 'shadow' the art folks to scout out an opportunity. I was approached by a paper conservator at a digital humanities workshop. The task of identifying pieces of antique handmade laid paper made on the same mold from the impression in the paper left by the screen in the mold was proposed to me as being similar to thread counting and worth my consideration. At that time the standard approach to identifying moldmates was to match watermarks. But only about a third of, for example, Rembrandt's prints have a watermark or a fragment of one in the paper. But all laid paper exhibits chain lines. We decided to see if a simple description of the chain line pattern was enough to guide reduction of a library of paper samples to a manageable number of candidate matches.

Therefore, we skipped development of an automatic chain line marker, which is a difficult problem that will ultimately need to be solved in a real system, in order to get more quickly to testing the hypothesis of moldmate candidate discovery using just the chain line pattern. We observed that many paper samples had straight but non-parallel chain lines, which for some reason was a combination that had not been studied in the thin literature on automating moldmate identification for antique laid papers. From there a least squares fit did the trick. That was enough to establish the feasibility of using chain line spacing sequences to help find laid paper moldmate candidates.

A big issue was that the data to which we had gained access was collected for looking at watermarks. Thus, the images were taken of just a small part of the full print. Consequently, they typically contained too few chain lines. The chain line sequences were often just not long enough to be unique enough to sufficiently reduce the percentage of false matches. We needed full-print images of the prints. Luckily, last year we gained access to a trove of indexed full print images of etchings by Rembrandt. We should have much to report by the end of this year.

Computational Art History or Digital Art History

PD – Why do you call what you do a part of "Computational Art History" rather than "Digital Art History"?

RJ – I'm mimicking the currently fashionable use of "computational" as in computational biology or chemistry or fluid dynamics or linguistics. I want to imply that it's not just sorting and displaying images in large datasets, which is what is implied to me – perhaps incorrectly – by the label "digital art history". It's now much more than just managing digitized datasets. It extends to extracting information from the images, both forensic and contextual. It's modeling and simulation. Recently, I've begun to interpret most of the problems of current interest in applying signal processing to computational art history as some form of image feature mining.

PD – Feature mining?

RJ – Yeah – you see that article.

Rick points to his desktop where he has laid out an article with "image feature mining" in its title by researchers using facial recognition as their application.

RJ – The big deal with this paper is that the algorithm didn't know what features to look for ahead of time. It came up with the interesting features itself. In many of our problems the feature of interest is defined in the problem statement. The issue is locating/extracting/measuring this feature automatically.

PD – Do you think that is a direction for Computational Art History?

RJ – Yes. But, again, if the problems and questions being answered aren't coming from the art community – it's not going to be adopted.

PD – What is the biggest impediment to showing you can be of value?

RJ – Still I think it is typically the lack of quality data in sufficient quantities. But, this is definitely starting to change. In the beginning I had to use images they already had gathered. And very few were digitized in 2006. Conservation departments didn't have their own scanners. It took too many resources to digitize large numbers of images. You have to figure out what they can actually provide – can you get enough data to get started and convincingly demonstrate a potential positive impact by what you are developing? We managed to get enough and get something going. Data is everything. That's why one of my targets has been convincing museums to provide easy access to academic researchers of more and more images of art objects.

PD – Let's imagine that that the floodgates open up and the data issue fades – where do you see the future of computational art history going?

RJ – Rather than try to make long-term projections, I'll relate a recent relevant experi-

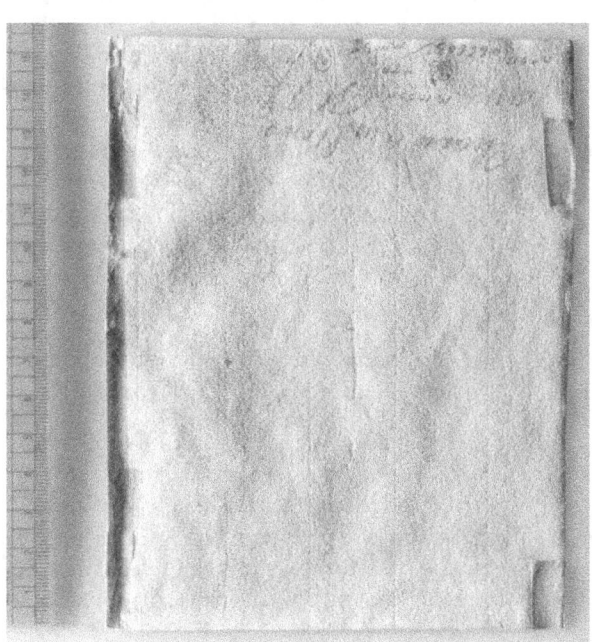

Vertical chain line impressions visible in raking light image of the back side of a Rembrandt etching "The Small Lion Hunt (with Two Lions)" on laid paper.
(Photo: David O. Brown/Herbert F. Johnson Museum of Art, Cornell University)
[For further details refer to C. R. Johnson, Jr. and others, "Hunting for Paper Moldmates Among Rembrandt's Prints," IEEE Signal Processing Magazine (Special Issue on Signal Processing for Art Investigation), (July 2015).]

"Newly institutionalized interactions are forming with art historians, curators, conservators, and engineers."

ence. As a guest editor for a forthcoming special issue of the IEEE Signal Processing Magazine on art investigation, I was trying to draft our editorial foreword about how what we are doing now in this nascent field relates to activity at the start of the 21st century when fewer signal processors were involved. I decided to divide the activities into image acquisition, manipulation, and feature mining. After consultation with my fellow guest editors, we decided that all of the articles in the special issue dealt with aspects of feature mining. Here we are using an inclusive definition of feature mining encompassing situations where the features are prescribed as well as instances where they are to be learned automatically – with a common primary objective being classification. This emphasis on feature mining contrasts sharply with the strong emphasis on image acquisition and manipulation around 2000. The current range of feature mining applications is quite broad, as evidenced by the topics addressed in the special issue, which include classifying ancient coins, facial recognition in Renaissance paintings, extracting and comparing visual stylistic features of paintings by a particular artist or school of artists, canvas thread counting, photographic and laid paper classification, and content based image indexing.

Imagine offering an art historian automatic labeling of content information in art works covering an artist's entire output – who knows what kinds of questions they would then ask? This is where I run out of my ability to predict the future. Uncertainty about the most fruitful future directions in such a young interdisciplinary field is a major reason for maintaining active cross-disciplinary collaborations in such projects. The domain is rich enough that I am convinced that some useful knowledge nuggets no one knows about now are waiting to be discovered. Thread counting and the subsequent weave density maps, thread angle maps, and roll layout capabilities form my current best example for this optimism.

PD – If the data is there...

RJ – Precisely! I think we are going to get to giant databases for images – I definitely think that is the direction. You'll load yours up to the cloud and within minutes you'll get a bunch of suggestions back about its mates. That's within reach. Within a decade, maybe. That should be a major target for our current collaborations. Again, my sense is not to try and predict – but get the data there and then we will see what happens – things I can't even guess now! Studying these mountains of data with feature mining tools seems like a very promising path to take.

PD – How do you see your contributions to this new field?

RJ – When I started I made a list of things that I wanted to accomplish. I wanted to convince more signal processors to look at these art investigation tasks. I wanted to convince art historians, curators, and conservators that the results from the signal processors will extend the scholarly reach of the art experts. I wanted to help establish an accessible archive of data and algorithms. I wanted to produce one textbook for both undergraduate engineers and graduate art and conservation students. And I wanted to give away software with a short course to conservation grad students. Basically, all of these targets were adopted as measures of my desire to accelerate the integration of signal processing and art history. All of these targets are now in hand or in sight.

I am very heartened – newly institutionalized interactions are forming with art historians, curators, conservators, and engineers all together at the start of interdisciplinary projects. The Netherlands Institute for Conservation, Art and Science and the Yale Lens Media Lab are recently inaugurated examples I have watched at close range as they took shape. I sit back sometimes and I think – it's really happening!

Sunshine is visible through the office's small window.

C. Richard Johnson, Jr. received a PhD in Electrical Engineering from Stanford University, along with the first PhD minor in Art History granted by Stanford, in 1977. Following 4 years on the faculty at Virginia Tech, he joined the Cornell University faculty in 1981, where he is the Geoffrey S. M. Hedrick Senior Professor of Engineering and a Stephen H. Weiss Presidential Fellow.

At the start of 2007, after 30 years of research on adaptive feedback systems theory and blind equalization in communication receivers, he accepted a 5-year appointment as an Adjunct Research Fellow of the Van Gogh Museum (Amsterdam, the Netherlands) to facilitate the interaction of art historians and conservation specialists with algorithm-building signal processors. In 2013, Professor Johnson was appointed a Scientific Researcher of the Rijksmuseum (Amsterdam, the Netherlands) and Computational Art History Advisor to the RKD - Netherlands Institute for Art History (the Hague, the Netherlands).

For a fuller description of Rick Johnson's research activities in computational art history, specifically using signal processing to match manufactured patterns in art supports, visit http://people.ece.cornell.edu/johnson/.

Park Doing earned B.S. and M. Eng. Degrees in Electrical Engineering and a Ph.D. in Science and Technology Studies, all from Cornell University. His book *Velvet Revolution at the Synchrotron: Physics, Biology and Change in Science* (MIT Press, 2009) analyzes interdisciplinary interactions between scientific fields, and between scientists and technicians. His subsequent research has centered on engineers as experts in dialogue with policymakers and the public. Most recently, he is focusing on applications of algorithmic processing to social issues and the humanities. He is currently a Lecturer in The Bovay Program in History and Ethics of Engineering at Cornell.

Quantitative Approaches

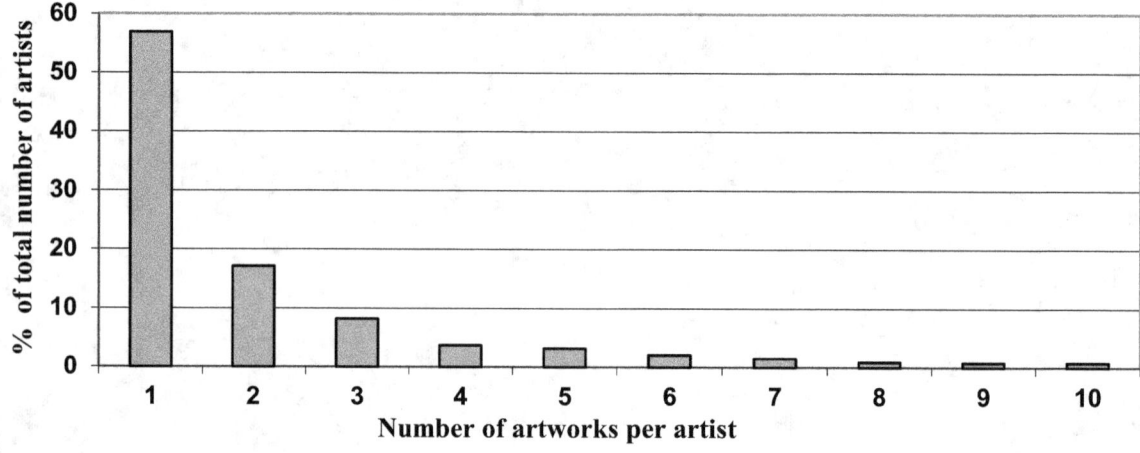

Figure 1: Plot of the number of artworks per artist in sample 1

Distant Viewing in Art History
A Case Study of Artistic Productivity

K. Bender

Abstract: With reference to the concept of distant reading in literary history, distant viewing is a valuable analogy for a quantitative approach to art history. In this case study of artistic productivity eight samples are analyzed, extracted from a digital thematic research collection about the iconography of Aphrodite/Venus from the Middle Ages to Modern Times. The result is an empirical finding of regularity never before highlighted in art history. The artistic productivity fits perfectly the distribution known as Lotka's law of scientific productivity in bibliographic science. Issues of collecting and sampling are discussed and the meaning of this empirical finding is hinted. Suggestions for future research are made.

Keywords: artistic/scientific productivity, distant reading/viewing, Lotka, quantitative art history

Introduction[1]

The French philosopher Michel Tournier[2] discusses the difference between quantity and quality and cites a quotation:

Sans doute la qualité vaut mieux que la quantité, mais sur la qualité,
on peut discuter à l'infini, tandis que la quantité, elle, est indiscutable.
Edward Reinrot[3]

Franco Moretti[4], who initiated the concept of 'distant reading' in literary history, made the same statement in other words: "Quantitative research provides a type of data which is ideally independent of interpretations...". Moretti argues that literature isn't a 'sum of individual cases', but a 'collective system'. Scholars have focused on a select group of texts: the canon. In 'distant reading' the canon disappears into the larger literary system.

These arguments are equally valuable for art history, where traditionally 'quality' matters more than 'quantity' and monographs focus predominantly on works considered as the great masterpieces of art. However, quantitative data such as the number of replicas, of engravings and subsequent duplications or imitations by other artists are gaining greater attention, and studies about the economics and market related aspects of art production are increasingly popular. The analysis of the spreading and popularity of motifs and style also requires 'numbers'.

This quantitative aspect of art history needs specific types of data acquisition. Structured data collections, alongside standard bibliographies, are crucial for advanced quantitative studies[5].

Reference works and reports provide evidence about the increasing importance of quantitative data, generating new forms of knowledge in the digital age of art history[6]. They can be analyzed computationally, as demonstrated for example in the pioneering work of Schich and Ebert-Schifferer[7], a trend following innovative research in literary history and therefore termed 'distant viewing in art history'.

This paper presents a case study about artistic productivity with a distribution known in bibliographic science as Lotka's law. All data, extracted from a digital thematic research collection, have been published and are freely available. Hence, the results presented in this paper are verifiable and the data could be used to explore alternative models of productivity in art history.

The case study

The productivity in terms of number of artworks created by an artist has been examined with the help of eight samples. The samples are taken from a digital thematic research collection compiled for a project of topical catalogues of the iconography of the Greek-Roman goddess Aphrodite/Venus, depicted in sculptures, paintings, drawings, prints and illustrations from the Middle Ages to Modern Times[8]. The topical categorization in these catalogues is mutually exclusive: no work is listed more than once. This methodology allows for quantitative analyses of the popularity of topics, of the time distributions of works and artists and of the number of works per artist[9].

In the first sample of 1840 works by 649 identified Italian artists, the average number of works per artist is 2,8. However, the counting of works per artist shows a very unequal 'productivity': a large majority (57 %) of all artists created only one 'Venus'-work in a lifetime, only 17 % made two works, 8% made three works, 3,5% made four works, 3% made five works, 2% made six works, etc. ... 0,8% made 10 works as shown in Fig.1 (number of works per artist on the horizontal axis and percentage number of artists on the vertical axis)[10].

All other samples in this project yield identical distributions as explained below. This empirical finding has never before been highlighted in art history.

Analogy with Lotka's law of scientific productivity

The American statistician Alfred J. Lotka published in the Journal of Washington Academy of Science, 1926, an article 'The frequency distribution of scientific productivity' based on an analysis of publications by authors in two fields of the exact sciences. Potter[11] reveals "...that Lotka's article was not cited until 1941, that his distribution was not termed "Lotka's law" until 1949, and that no attempts were made to test the applicability of Lotka's law to other disciplines until 1973'.

Lotka found that the number of authors producing x publications is about

$$1/x^a$$

of those making one publication, or:

$$y = C/x^a$$

where y is the relative frequency (or proportional number) of authors with x publications and the constant C and the exponent a are parameters. Thus for $x = 1$, $C = y$.

This is an inverse power function, now commonly referred to as 'Lotka's law'[12]. Lotka suggested that the exponent a nearly always equals 2 and the function can then be called an inverse square function. This means that the number of

Figure 2: Observed frequencies of number of works per artist and fitted inverse power equation for Sample 1
$y = 0{,}6222\ x^{-1{,}948}\ \ R^2 = 0{,}9929$

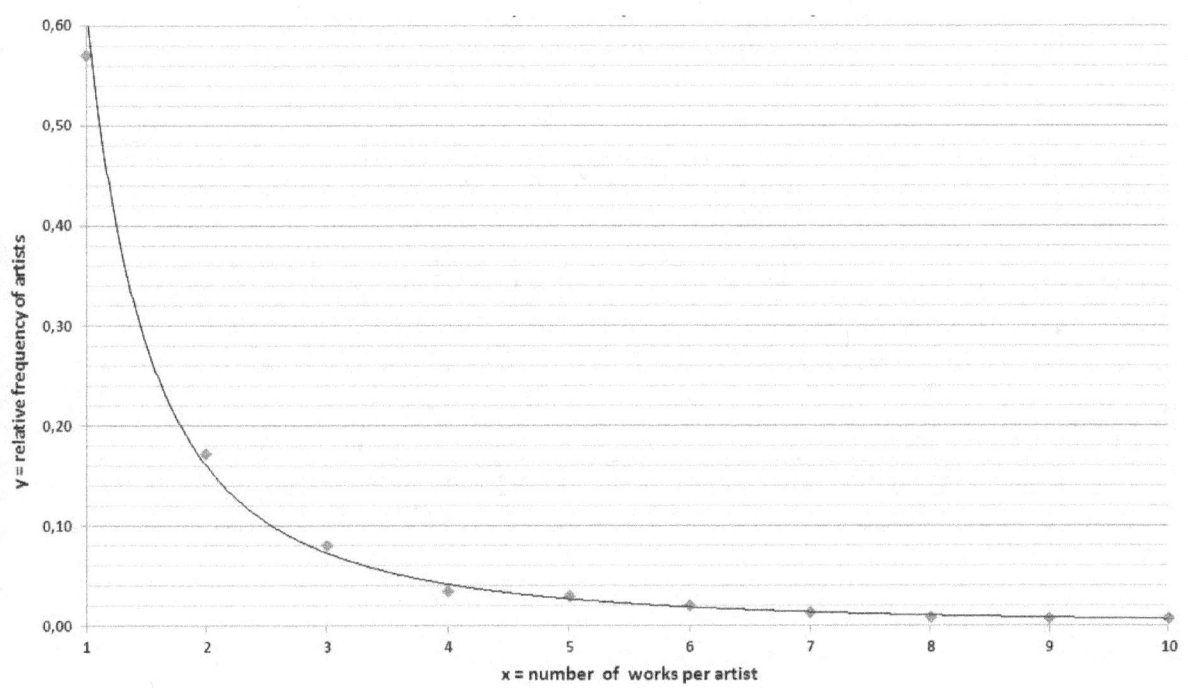

authors making 2 publications is *1 / 2*2 = 1 / 4 = 0.25* of those making 1 publication; those making 3 publications: *1 / 3*3 = 1 / 9 = 0.11* of those making 1 publication, etc. This surprisingly resembles the distribution as shown in Fig.1. Hence, it was a logic step to try out Lotka's law with the data of our first sample. By logarithmic transformation of the data and using the classical linear regression technique or 'least squares method', applied for instance automatically in the trend-line functionality in 'charts' of Microsoft Office Excel 2007, we can estimate the values of the parameters:

$$C = 0{,}6222 \text{ and } a = 1{,}948$$

and calculate a goodness-of-fit measure between the equation and the observed data, commonly called the correlation coefficient R^2 (with $0 < R^2 < 1$; the closer R^2 is to *1*, the better fit):

$$R^2 = 0{,}9929$$

Thus the result of this test, plotted in Fig.2, shows a close resemblance to Lotka's law with an exponent *a* very near to the suggested value 2^{13}.

Further evidence for all samples

The next step was to analyze the data of all samples in the project compiled with the same methodology as sample 1. The data are extracted from the publications by Bender[14]. The basic data (*N* = total number of artists; *X* = total number of works; x = X/N average number of works per artist) for the eight samples are presented in Table 1 and the observed data of number *n* of artworks and relative frequency *y* of artists for each sample are given in Table 2.

Table 1: Basic data of the samples
(N = total number of artists; X = total number of works; average number of works x = X/N)

sample	N	X	x	country of artist's origin	references
1	649	1840	2,8	Italy	9a
2	977	2997	3,1	France	9b
3	728	2636	3,6	Low Countries	9c
4	1506	3198	2,1	Germany, Switzerland, Central-Europe	9d
5	912	2113	2,3	Great Britain, Ireland	9e
6	184	291	1,5	Eastern Region	9f
7	220	503	2,3	Southern Region	
8	215	577	2,7	Northern Region	
total	5401	14155	2,6		

Table 2: Observed data of the samples
(x = number of works created by an artist; n = number of artists who created x works; relative frequency of artists who created x works: y = x/N; N = total number of artists)

sample		\multicolumn{10}{c}{x}									
		1	2	3	4	5	6	7	8	9	10
1	n	371	112	53	23	20	14	9	6	5	5
	y	0,5716	0,1726	0,0817	0,0354	0,0308	0,0216	0,0139	0,0092	0,0077	0,0077
2	n	586	158	75	31	28	19	11	8	9	9
	y	0,5998	0,1617	0,0768	0,0317	0,0286	0,0194	0,0112	0,0082	0,0092	0,0092
3	n	398	122	52	30	29	19	7	8	12	4
	y	0,5467	0,1676	0,0714	0,0412	0,0398	0,0261	0,0096	0,0110	0,0165	0,0055
4	n	1027	215	95	53	34	27	7	10	6	6
	y	0,6819	0,1428	0,0631	0,0352	0,0226	0,0179	0,0046	0,0066	0,0040	0,0040
5	n	628	119	65	25	20	10	7	4	4	5
	y	0,6886	0,1305	0,0713	0,0274	0,0219	0,0110	0,0077	0,0044	0,0044	0,0055
6	n	148	20	12	7	1	0	1	0	0	0
	y	0,7629	0,1031	0,0619	0,0361	0,0052	0,0000	0,0052	0,0000	0,0000	0,0000
7	n	162	30	12	7	2	1	2	1	1	0
	y	0,7364	0,1364	0,0545	0,0318	0,0091	0,0045	0,0091	0,0045	0,0045	0,0000
8	n	139	32	12	8	6	2	4	3	1	2
	y	0,6465	0,1488	0,0558	0,0372	0,0279	0,0093	0,0186	0,0140	0,0047	0,0093
all	n	3459	808	376	184	140	92	48	40	38	31
	y	0,6404	0,1496	0,0696	0,0341	0,0259	0,0170	0,0089	0,0074	0,0070	0,0057

The estimated values of the parameters C and a and the calculated goodness-of-fit measure R^2 for the individual samples vary between 0,5675 and 0,7506 for C, 1,865 and 2,264 for a, and 0,9423 and 0,9929 for R^2. The computation for all samples merged (last row in Table 2) yields:

$$y = 0,6505 / x^{2,089} \text{ with } R^2 = 0,9945$$

The estimated value of the constant C = 0,65 is near the observed value y = 0,64 and the value of the exponent a = 2,089 is again very close to the value suggested by Lotka and thus the proposed inverse power function is practically an inverse square law (Fig. 3).

In this exercise the number of x has been deliberately limited to 10. However, it is known that observations of large values of x do not fit well the Lotka distribution: the so-called 'long-tail' problem. Therefore, an alternative model with three parameters was applied for samples 1, 2 and 3 when all values of x were included in the computations[15]. Though the model yielded slightly better goodness-of-fit measures R^2, the values of C and a were not longer comparable among samples due to interaction with the third parameter and the model was discarded.

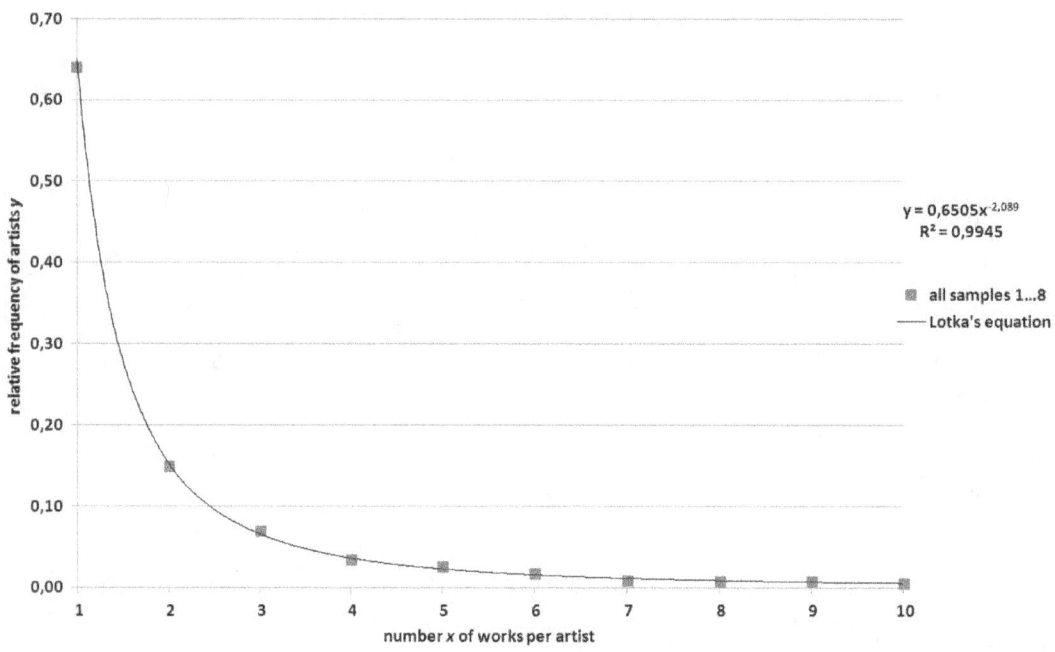

Figure 3: Observations and Lotka's law for all samples 1...8

Discussion of results

The perfect fit, with a very high value of the goodness-of-fit measure $R^2 = 0,9945$, to a large set of samples representing in total 14155 artworks, created over a period of more than 500 years by 5401 artists from all over Europe, leaves no doubt that the so-called "Lotka's law of scientific productivity" is applicable to this case study of art historical data. However, the sampling method, the thematic collection, the Lotka distribution and its 'long tail', and the meaning of the empirical finding, are issues deserving discussion and further study.

- The sampling method in this case study is not 'at random' where all artworks would have equal chance to be selected in the 'population' of the indefinite number of artworks by an unknown number of artists of a thematic research collection. In fact, the sampling is a 'convenient' one and always biased in a thematic collection because many artworks, never recorded, were lost and the information sources are limited to the collector. Hence, the representativeness and the size of the samples are always issues. The samples in this case study are presumably very large[16]; nevertheless their size can be always enlarged[17]. An advanced study of the sampling bias will eventually be performed in the future through methods of meta-analysis[18].

- More important are the formal concept of a thematic collection and its methodology of topical categorization: indeed, the series created form the basis for the distant viewing concept. Therefore, the series should be as homogeneous as possible in order to make quantification possible[19]. The fact that there is a remarkable regularity in all samples of this case study is an indication that the homogeneity of the thematic collection is high.

- Why does scientific/artistic productivity not follow the 'normal' Gaussian distribution of events that go by chance? Gaussian distribution offers an 'equal' chance to each event. Lotka's law, on the contrary, shows a very 'unequal' situation: 65% of the sources (authors/ artists) produce only 1 item (publication/work) and relatively few sources produce many items. The few artists producing more than 10 works in this case study – i.e. the so-called 'long tail' in the distribution – are, however, not the least known: on the contrary, many well-known masters are among the most prolific 'Venus'-artists[20]. No doubt, this is related to problems of authenticity and attribution of the artworks as well as to the issue of workshop management of the production.

- Egghe[21] discusses at length the principle of 'success breeds success' or 'cumulative advantage' and demonstrates mathematically how it is related to Lotka's equation. The phenomenon is comparable to the economic or financial rule: 'the richer you are, the easier to get even richer'. One can interpret this as follows for the case study: there is always a probability that an artist with no 'Venus'-work in the past will create a first one. If this first 'Venus'-work has success, the greater probability will be that the artist will produce another 'Venus'-work and so on; if, however, this first work is a failure or has no success, the artist will probably not create a second 'Venus'-work. This may explain the high value of *y = 65% for x = 1* as well as the 'long tail' phenomenon of superstar artists with a large network of patrons and customers. This case study provides quantitative data for socio-economic models of creativity as discussed by Menger[22].

- In his search to find an interpretation of Lotka's law, Price discusses the basic difference between creative effort in the sciences and in the arts: "The artist's creation is intensively personal, whereas that of the scientist needs recognition by his peers"[23]. Authorship of scientific articles is therefore an indication of prestige. The finding in this case study seems to prove that this distinction is mistaken: the artistic creativity follows a similar pattern as the scientific effort and obviously has also everything to do with 'prestige'. Moreover, the way how modern research is funded through targeted programs has some similarity with preferences of art patrons and fashion on the art market.

Conclusion and suggestions for future research

The empirical finding of this case study is remarkable and its interpretation 'success breeds success' has never been highlighted before in art history. The 'distant viewing' approach of a fairly homogeneous thematic collection and the quantification of data in eight large independent samples proves successful and could be an example for future quantitative research in art history. Are there other thematic collections in art history available which comply with the conditions of homogeneity and size? If yes, then one could further test the applicability of Lotka's law for other themes or explore more sophisticated models. A better understanding of the underlying regularity could give rise to unorthodox questions and offer new ways to decipher the complexity of artistic productivity.

Notes

[1] The author gratefully acknowledges the helpful comments of the anonymous peer-reviewers of the draft paper. He also thanks Paul Taylor of The Warburg Institute, London, for discussion of Fig.1 and for drawing his attention to the analogy with Lotka's law, and Béatrice Joyeux-Prunel of the Ecole Normale Supérieure, Paris, for her support regarding socio-economic reference material.

[2] Michel Tournier, "Quantité et qualité" in Le miroir des idées – Traité (Paris : Mercure de France, 1995), 205-208.

[3] Author's translation: 'Without doubt quality is better than quantity, but quality can be discussed ad infinitum, while quantity is indisputable'. Edward Reinrot is a pseudonym of Tournier himself.

[4] Franco Moretti, Graphs, Maps, Trees – Abstract models for literary history (London, New York: Verso, 2007) 9.

[5] Among many online data collections, such as 'Bildindex Foto Marburg' http://www.bildindex.de and 'The Warburg Institute Iconographic Database' http://warburg.sas.ac.uk/photographic-collection/iconographic-database/ of a general nature, one can also cite some specific ones: * the 'Census of Antique Works of Art and Architecture known in the Renaissance', started in 1947 at the Warburg Institute, University of London, and online http://www.census.de * the 'Montias Database of 17th Century Dutch Art Inventories', developed in the '80s by the economist John Michael Montias, online at the Frick Art Reference Library http://research.frick.org/montias/home.php

[6] Béatrice Joyeux-Prunel, éd., L' Art et la Mesure - Histoire de l'art et méthodes quantitatives: sources, outils, bonnes pratiques. (Paris: Editions Rue d'Ulm, 2010) https://ens.academia.edu/B%C3%A9atriceJoyeuxPrunel/Books. Hubertus Kohle, Digitale Bildwissenschaft. (Glückstadt, Verlag Werner Hülsbusch, 2013). http://archiv.ub.uni-heidelberg.de/artdok/2185/1/Kohle_Digitale_Bildwissenschaften_2013.pdf. Matthew Long and Roger C. Schonfeld, Supporting the Changing Research Practices of Art Historians. (Ithaka S+R, 2014) http://www.sr.ithaka.org/sites/default/files/reports/SR_Support-Changing-Research-ArtHist_20140429.pdf

[7] Maximilian Schich and Sybille Ebert-Schifferer, Bildkonstruktionen bei Annibale Carracci and Caravaggio: Analyse von kunstwissenschaftlichen Datenbanken mit Hilfe skalierbarer Bildmatrizen (ART-Dok report, 2008) http://archiv.ub.uni-heidelberg.de/artdok/volltexte/2009/712

[8] About the relevance of the motif of Aphrodite/Venus in Western art history, the author refers to reference Caroline Arscott and Katia Scott, eds., Manifestations of Venus – Art and sexuality. (Manchester and New York: Manchester University Press, 2000).

[9] Details in several posts and especially in the series 'Statistics in Art History' in the author's Blog 'Iconography in Art History' http://kbender.blogspot.be/?view=magazine

[10] For practical reasons of visualization the graph is limited to 10 artworks per artist. See below about the 'long-tail' issue.

[11] William Gray Potter, "*Lotka's Law Revisited*"; Library Trends 31,2 (1981)): 21-39. https://www.ideals.illinois.edu/bitstream/handle/2142/7191/librarytrendsv30i1e_opt.pdf?sequence=1#page=1&zoom=auto,-87,590

[12] It would be better called 'Lotka's equation or distribution' since it is not a precise law, a term used in physics.

[13] The more exact 'maximum likelihood method' to estimate the parameters C and a yields similar results for all numbers x: $C = 0,6095$ and $a = 2,0047$. Details on the author's webpage *'LOTKA's Law of Productivity'* https://sites.google.com/site/venusiconography/home/research-papers/lotka-s-law-of-productivity

[14] K. Bender: The Iconography of Venus from the Middle Ages to Modern Times. Volumes 1.1 to 6.1. (2007, 2009, 2010, 2012, 2013, 2014). Physical books published by www.lulu.com and www.shopmybook.com/en/, https://archive.org/search.php?query=K.%20bender%20Venus%20AND%20mediatype%3Atexts

[15] K. Bender, "Time Distribution, Popularity, Diversity and Productivity of the Iconography of Venus in the Low Countries, France and Italy", Research Paper 5 in the Series 'Quantitative Iconography of Venus' (2011) https://independent.academia.edu/KBender/Papers

[16] For comparison reasons: a search "Venus since the 6th century" in the above cited general collections 'Bildindex Foto Marburg' and 'The Warburg Institute Iconographic Database' yields, respectively, 5406 and 2699 images, all attributions confounded.

[17] This would especially be useful for samples 6, 7 and 8. The author is presently revising the Topical Catalogue 'The Italian Venus' (reference 9a), leading to a much larger sample which then can be used for a meta-analysis.

[18] John E. Hunter and Frank L. Schmidt, Methods of Meta-Analysis – Correcting Error and Bias in Research Findings. (Thousand Oaks: SAGE Publications, 2004).

[19] General collections like the ones quoted above do not easily allow to quantification because thematic search terms in the database do not necessarily retrieve mutually exclusive artworks, i.e. the same artwork can be retrieved more than once. The same problem occurs in standard thematic reference works like Pigler's 'Barock-Themen' or the Oxford Guide to 'Classical Mythology in the Arts, 1300-1990s', both unfortunately not yet digitized.

[20] See author's post of March 27, 2014 'The Venus of the Eastern, Southern and Northern European Regions' http://kbender.blogspot.be/2014/03/the-venus-of-eastern-southern-and.html

[21] Leo Egghe, Power laws in the information production process: Lotkaian informetrics. (Oxford: Elsevier, 2005) 45. http://yunus.hacettepe.edu.tr/~tonta/courses/spring2011/bby704/power%20laws%20in%20information%20production%20processes-e-book-qvt7lUnRLk.pdf

[22] Pierre-Michel Menger, The Economics of Creativity – Art and Achievement under Uncertainty. (Cambridge, Mass: Harvard University Press, 2014), 179f, 274 inter alia.

[23] Derek J. De Solla Price, Little Science Big Science. (New York: Columbia University Press, 1963), 69.

Bibliography

1. Tournier, Michel. *Le miroir des idées – Traité*. Paris: Mercure de France, 1995. 269 pp.
2. Moretti, Franco. *Graphs, Maps, Trees – Abstract models for literary history*. London, New York: Verso, 2007. 119 pp.
3. Joyeux-Prunel, Béatrice, editeur. *L' Art et la Mesure - Histoire de l' art et méthodes quantitatives : sources, outils, bonnes pratiques*. Paris: Editions Rue d'Ulm, 2010. 600 pp. https://ens.academia.edu/B%C3%A9atrice JoyeuxPrunel/Books
4. Kohle, Hubertus. *Digitale Bildwissenschaft*. Glückstadt, Verlag Werner Hülsbusch, 2013. 189 pp. http://archiv.ub.uni-heidelberg.de/artdok/2185/1/Kohle_Digitale_Bildwissenschaften_2013.pdf
5. Long, Matthew and Roger C. Schonfeld. *Supporting the Changing Research Practices of Art Historians*. USA, Ithaka S+R, 2014. 54 pp. http://www.sr.ithaka.org/sites/default/files/reports/SR_Support-Changing-

Research-ArtHist_20140429.pdf

6. Schich, Maximilian and Sybille Ebert-Schifferer. *Bildkonstruktionen bei Annibale Carracci and Caravaggio: Analyse von kunstwissenschaftlichen. Databanken mit Hilfe skalierbarer Bildmatrizen.* Digital Repository Art History: ART-Dok report. http://archiv.ub.uni-heidelberg.de/artdok/volltexte/2009/712
7. Arscott, Caroline and Katia Scott, editors. *Manifestations of Venus – Art and sexuality.* Manchester and New York: Manchester University Press, 2000. 233 pp.
8. Potter, William Gray. "Lotka's Law Revisited". *Library Trends* 31,2 (1981): 21-39. https://www.ideals.illinois.edu/bitstream/handle/2142/7191/librarytrendsv30i1e_opt.pdf?sequence=1#page=1&zoom=auto,-87,590
9. Bender, K. *The Iconography of Venus from the Middle Ages to Modern Times.*
   9a. Vol. 1.1 'The Italian Venus' (2007) 156 pp.
   9b. Vol. 2.1 'The French Venus' (2009) 194 pp.
   9c. Vol. 3.1 'The Venus of the Low Countries' (2010) 202 pp.
   9d. Vol. 4.1 'The German, Swiss and Central-European Venus' (2012) 302 pp.
   9e. Vol. 5.1 'The British and Irish Venus' (2013) 197 pp.
   9f. Vol. 6.1 'The Venus of the Eastern, Southern and Northern European Regions' (2014) 154 pp.
Physical books published by www.lulu.com and www.shopmybook.com/en/ https://archive.org/search.php?query=K.%20bender%20Venus%20AND%20mediatype%3Atexts
10. Bender, K. *Time Distribution, Popularity, Diversity and Productivity of the Iconography of Venus in the Low Countries, France and Italy. Research Paper 5 in the Series 'Quantitative Iconography of Venus'.* 26 pp. https://independent.academia.edu/KBender/Papers
11. Hunter, John E. and Frank L. Schmidt. *Methods of Meta-Analysis – Correcting Error and Bias in Research Findings.* Thousand Oaks: SAGE Publications, 2004. 582 pp.
12. Egghe, Leo. *Power laws in the information production process: Lotkaian informetrics.* Oxford: Elsevier, 2005. 447 pp. http://yunus.hacettepe.edu.tr/~tonta/courses/spring2011/bby704/power%20laws%20in%20information%20 production%20processes-e-book-qvt7lUnRLk.pdf
13. Menger, Pierre-Michel. *The Economics of Creativity – Art and Achievement under Uncertainty.* Cambridge, Mass: Harvard University Press, 2014. 405 pp.
14. Price, Derek J. De Solla. *Little Science, Big Science.* New York: Columbia University Press, 1963. 119 pp.

K. Bender is an independent researcher in Belgium with an academic background in the 'hard' sciences and developing his digital thematic research collection since 2004.

Correspondence e-mail: bender@telenet.be
https://twitter.com/bender_k

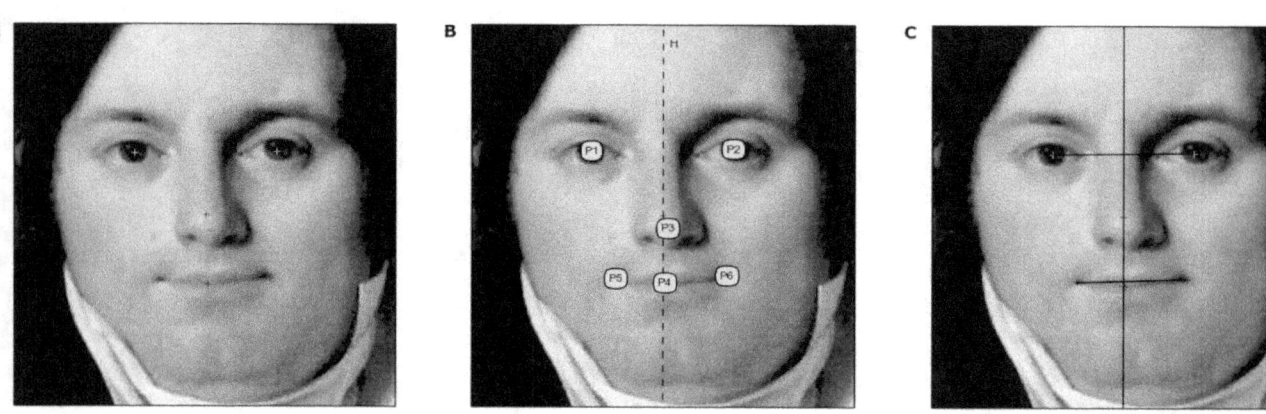

Figure 1: Steps for the calculation of the symmetry of a face.
(A) Example of face and detected points for eyes, nose, mouth and center.
(B) Vertical line, H, to divide the face into two hemi-faces, and enumerated points for all the features.
(C) Lines for calculating distances between midpoints and hemi-face line.

Peer-Reviewed

A Quantitative Approach to Beauty. Perceived Attractiveness of Human Faces in World Painting

Javier de la Rosa, Juan-Luis Suárez

Abstract: Has human beauty always been perceived in the same manner? We used a set of 120,000 paintings from different periods to analyze human faces between the 13th and the 20th centuries in order to establish whether there has been a single canon of beauty (that would maximize reproduction probabilities) or whether this has changed over time. Our study shows that when measuring averageness, symmetry, and orientation, the representation of human faces has not remained constant and that there are substantial differences between the faces depicted between the 15th and 18th centuries when compared to those of both the 13th and 20th centuries. Especially significant is the decrease in the perceived beauty of faces in 20th-century paintings, as the freedom of artists and the openness of society fostered the representation of different types of human faces other than that of classical styles.

Keywords: culturomics, digital humanities, beauty, facial recognition, computer vision

Introduction[1]

The voters who participated in the "2012 Britain's Most Beautiful Face" competition agreed on considering that Florence Colgate's face was the most beautiful one and named her the winner among 8,000 entries.[2] It turns out that the distance between her eyes and mouth is a 32% of her face, almost the exact third that Greeks considered to be the perfect proportion of a beautiful face. The results of this contest emphasized the long-standing human effort to scientifically estimate the features of beauty and to establish a method that allows for a reliable measurement of that which makes a face attractive.

The relation between the proportions of the human face and its perceived attractiveness have always captured attention and produced enormous fascination among scientists and artists alike. Even newborns seem to dedicate more time to attractive faces than to others.[3] How these proportions are meant to be the guidelines that define facial beauty has been the object of philosophic and scientific considerations since Plato's time. However, binary approaches to beauty, such as Hogarth's serpentine line,[4] the Vitruvius' "well-shaped man",[5] *divina proportione*, the golden ratio, or Fibonacci, have proven inconclusive to explain how beauty is actually perceived.[6] As it has been considered that expression of a face is the sum of a multitude of small details,[7] we can also say that the attractiveness of a face is the sum of a varied set of distinct features. The latest investigations on evolutionary psychology and neuro-aesthetics point at similar conclusions. Beauty of unknown faces seems to include elements from averageness, symmetry, sexual dimorphism, pleasant expressions, and youthfulness.[8] While the existence of universal beauty standards should be explained in terms of an adaptionist approach to attractiveness, these standards should vary across cultures if they are the result of esthetic judgments or culturally dependent values.[9]

The goal of setting the exact measurements that would help us establish the degree of beauty of a face suggests that these measures, and the beauty implicit in them, respond to the existence of a stereotype of physical attractiveness and that this stereotype might have remained constant throughout human history, even if it is a byproduct of the perceptual system's design and not the result of evolved psychological adaptations.[10] That is, a face that was considered beautiful during the Renaissance would have also been attractive in the Baroque, Neoclassical or Modernist periods. And the reverse would also be true: faces that are considered beautiful today such as those of Brad Pitt, Angelina Jolie, or Johnny Depp would have been among the most attractive faces in centuries past. These would be timeless beauties. But, is this really the case? Can we infer that the astonishing resemblance of Scarlett Johansson to the woman depicted in Vermeer's *Girl with a Pearl Earring* is due to the existence of a constant canon of beauty in human history?

Given the abundance of data required to carry out a study that comprises as many periods and genres of art history as possible, we decided to take the concept of beauty in a measurable and comparable way. We are aware that an objective definition of beauty might not necessarily correlate with the ideals of the artists and, therefore, the assumption that artists intend to represent beauty might be theoretically disputable. We do not make such an assumption. We try to establish to what extend the result of artists' practices converges or deviates from numerically measurable standards of beauty as understood by the scientific discourse. Because of methodological reasons, in our study, the focus is placed on the current standards of beauty as defined by scientific methodology in terms of face symmetry and averageness. These two indices seem to be related to the perception of beauty: symmetrical faces are the result of a non-problematic development after puberty, and therefore guarantee a better offspring.[11] Averageness, on the other hand, operates by the evolutionary pressure of Darwin's theory of natural selection: subjects with features close to the mean for a population are preferred to others, as the probability of them having harmful mutations is lower.[12] Therefore, there is enough evidence to support the idea that both symmetry and averageness play a role in the perception of beauty: the more average and symmetrical, the more beautiful a face is usually ranked. A perfect combination of the external criterion –relation to the average face of a period– and the internal criterion –symmetry of features– would result in the most attractive face, turning a subjective opinion such as what face is beautiful into something measurable and objective.

Coming up with the right set of faces in order to determine levels of beauty in various historical periods, was not a straightforward path. Nowadays, it is becoming less difficult to perform studies on faces thanks to the overflow of photographs that we come across on any given day. The combination of digital technologies, ubiquity of cell phones and cameras, and widespread distribution of information through social networks make it relatively easy to get hold of large data sets of faces on which to perform beauty analysis and validation.[13] However, before the official birth of practical photography in 1839 and its subsequent popularization in the 20th century, the only historical record available of human images was that of art history. Drawings and paintings have always been prone to representations of human figures. Both in the portraiture genre and as part of more diverse compositions, human faces can be found in numerous works of art of most styles and historical periods. The question is how to use the faces represented in paintings such as *Mona Lisa* by Leonardo Da Vinci, *Self-Portrait Without Beard* by Vincent van Gogh, or *The Night Watch* by Rembrandt as the subject of the type of analysis required to isolate features, measure distances, or determine metrics of averageness in a set of faces.

Materials and Methods

Surprisingly, the most extensive source of paintings, as well as the easiest to work with, came from a private collection of digital images curated for years and made available on-line for free.[14] Every painting has at least information about title, size, author, and date. However, accurate dates are only provided for paintings in the past two centuries– before the 1800s, the dataset only has the century in which the painting was produced (although some open collections have appeared more recently).[15] For this reason, we treated all paintings equally and decided to use the century information as the basic unit of time for this study. On the other hand, the resolution of the images of the paintings was not very important since face detection algorithms usually work by scaling high resolution images down. For the algorithm we used, images bigger than 1024px of height or width were resized before being processed.[16] We used a Python script to download the meta-data for each image, perform the requests to the face recognition API, and collect, clean and organize the results.[17] The algorithms for calculating symmetry and averageness indices were also written in Python, following the formulas detailed below.

Besides the calculation of the boundaries of a face and the position of several facial traits–such as eyes, nose, mouth, ears, or chin–, the algorithm we used also made guesses about the gender and age of the depicted faces, basing its estimations on the distribution and proportions of the traits and providing a threshold of confidence. Calculation of symmetry is commonly based on an early work of Grammer and Thornhill.[18] Their method makes use of 12 different points (one more for averageness): 2 for each eye, 2 for the nose, 2 for the mouth, 2 for the cheekbones, and the last 2 for the jaw. With these points, they create lines for each pair and calculate their midpoints. In a perfectly symmetrical face, all midpoints must lie on the same vertical line. For our study, the algorithm used is significantly more limited compared to that, with 3 points for the mouth (left, center, and right), 1 for each pupil, and 1 for the nose. We could have considered ears or chin, but the number of faces in which these attributes were found with enough

Figure 2: Average composites per century for female, both genders, and male. Each tuple of three images, starting from the rightmost side, represents the average composite of a given century for female, both genders, and male faces, respectively. These images were generated in order to calculate the values of averageness per century for each face. All-time composites are also available in SM as figure S1.

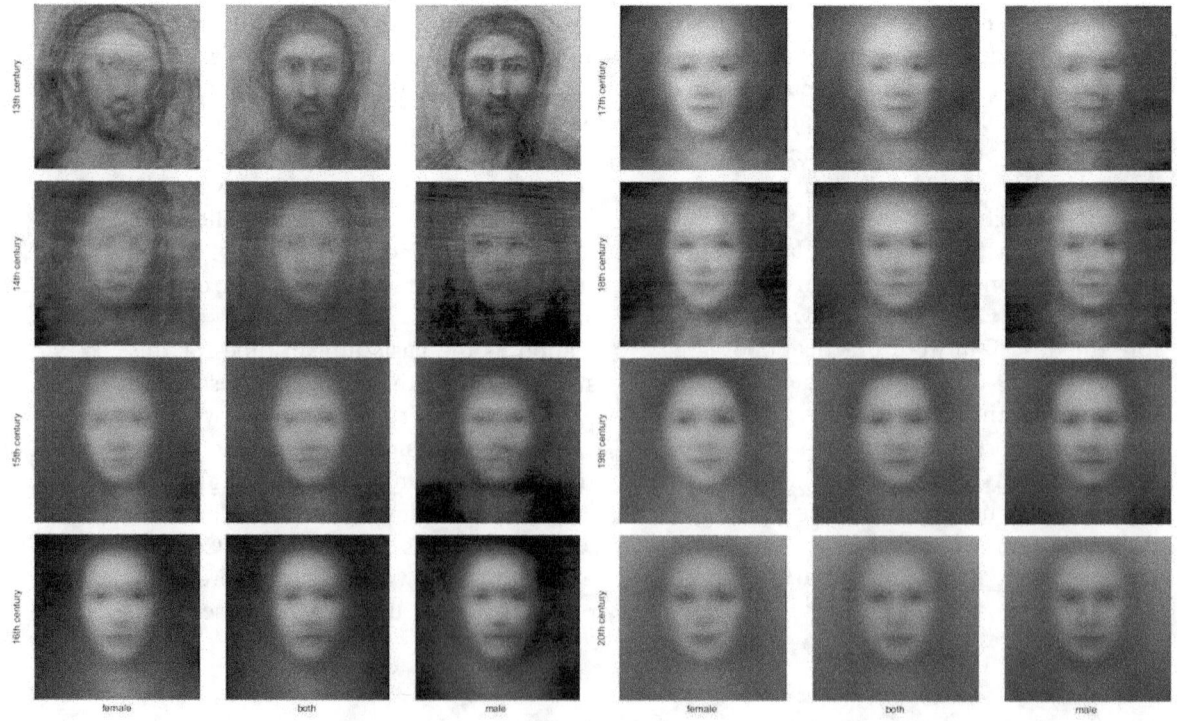

confidence (higher than 80%) is fairly insignificant (6%). Therefore, our method to calculate the symmetry of a face differs slightly from the one proposed by Grammer and Thornhill, while the main idea remains unchanged. Besides the points cited previously, the algorithm also gives us the centroid or geometric center of all detected features (Fig. 1A), which is supposed to coincide with the center of the face. From it, we can set a straight line that splits the face into two sides or hemi-faces. Figure 1B shows points 1 to 6 (P1 for left eye, P2 for right eye, P3 for nose, P4 for mouth center, P5 for left mouth corner, and P6 for right mouth corner), as well as the line H, that we assume to be the axis of face symmetry. We now trace segments: D1 between P1 and P2, and D2 between P5 and P6 (Fig. 1C). For these segments we calculate the midpoints M1 and M2. Symmetry is now obtained as the sum of the distances in pixels of M1, M2, P3 and P6 with respect to the line H. Only lateral symmetry is therefore estimated. For perfect symmetrical faces this value adds to zero; all symmetry values are normalized between 0 and 1, and we inverted the meaning to make plots clearer, where 1 means perfect symmetry, and 0 total asymmetry.

Let be ($center_x$, $center_y$) the point that defines the center of a face, and *roll* the rotation angle as returned by the algorithm, being 0° a perpendicular face with respect to the baseline of the frame of the painting. Then, we define the symmetry of face, Sym,[19] as follows:

$$Sym_{face} = 1 - \frac{Sym'_{face}}{max_{Sym'}} \quad (1)$$

$$Sym'_{face} = d_{H,M1} + d_{H,M2} + d_{H,P3} + d_{H,P6} \quad (2)$$

where the hemi-face line, H, defined as:

$$H = mx + k \quad (3)$$

$$m = tan(90 - roll) \quad (4)$$

$$k = center_y - m\,center_x \quad (5)$$

Formulas for the midpoints and the point to line distance are also described below:

$$M_{p1,p2} = (\frac{p1_x + p2_x}{2}, \frac{p1_y + p2_y}{2}) \quad (6)$$

$$d_{H,p} = \frac{|mp_x - p_y + k|}{\sqrt{(m^2+1)}} \quad (7)$$

On the other hand, the obtaining of averageness values involves a task much more demanding in terms of computer power. For each century an average face has been computer-generated for male, female and both (Fig. 2). In order to produce this averaged composite face, we first centered the faces according to the center point given by the face recognition algorithm. Faces were then resized to make them fit into a PNG canvas of 500 by 500 pixels at 300dpi of resolution, and given a height of 200 pixels; faces with height lower than 150 pixels were excluded to avoid blurred pixelation of the average face. This process was achieved by using affine and projective 2D transformations from the original painting to the desired canvas. Every face standardized by size was then converted into a 3D numerical matrix representing each of the layers of the RGB color model. A regular statistical mean was then calculated over the set of faces of each century in order to obtain the average value for each pixel. Once the average matrix was calculated, it was converted back into a PNG image. The resulting quality and averageness of the composite relied on the number of faces used in each century for generating the averaged face. The same face recognition algorithm used in the dataset was then applied on averaged composites. This allowed us to measure the averageness of an individual face as the difference between its symmetry and the symmetry of the average face for that particular period.

Let be F the set of k faces of a specific period of time, in our case, a century. Then we calculate the average composite as follows:

$$Avg_{face} = |Sym_{face} - Sym_{Comp}| \qquad (8)$$

$$F = \{face_1, \ldots, face_k\} \qquad (9)$$

$$Comp_F = \frac{1}{k}\sum_{i=0}^{k} face_i = \frac{1}{k}\sum_{i=0}^{k} \langle R_i, G_i, B_i \rangle \qquad (10)$$

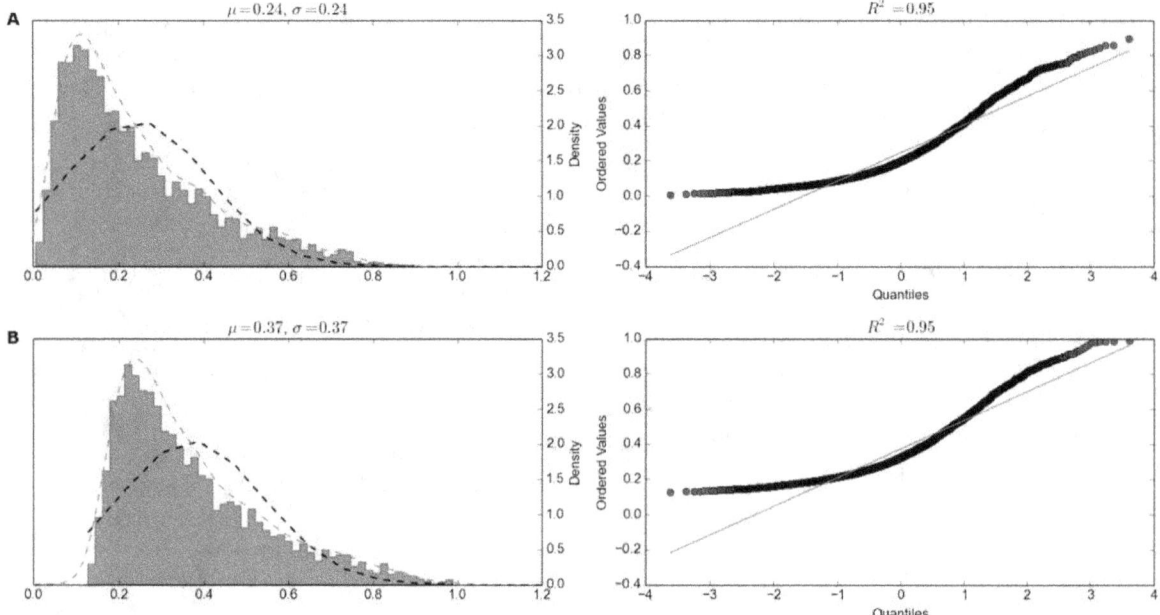

Figure 3: Normalized histograms (left) and Q-Q plots (right) for values of symmetry (A) and averageness (B). Gaussian density estimations are shown in dashed red lines, and probability density function estimations are shown in dashed black lines. Both distributions follow a normal distribution (p=3.31e-05 and p=3.68e-05, respectively, after running a KS test).

Averageness refers to the degree to which a given face resembles the majority of faces. In our study averageness values go from the most average, 1, to the least, 0. Figure 3, A and B, shows the histogram and the density estimation for the distributions of both symmetry and averageness values, respectively.

A considerable amount of paintings and faces were needed to draw valid conclusions about trends in human representation and facial attractiveness across historical periods. We retrieved and analyzed a data set with over 120,000 digital images of paintings covering styles and artistic periods spanning from the 13th to the 20th century. We applied face recognition algorithms to these images to remove all paintings that had no recognizable faces in them, to end up with 25,000 paintings and over 47,000 human faces. For the current study only 5,800 faces that fulfill the following criteria were considered: frontal faces no smaller than 150 pixels in height, with pitch and yaw angles between 20° and -20° with respect to the vertical line, and with valid information for at least the following traits: eyes, nose, mouth, height, width, and center of the face. Face rotation or roll was fixed geometrically. Once we had identified the traits of the detected faces, and based on meta-analysis of symmetry and averageness,[20] we were able to compare the beauty and attractiveness of faces in order to determine different trends and variations across time periods as they appeared in the history of painting.

A decline in perceived beauty

Average values of symmetry per century are shown in figure 4A for male, female, and both genders combined. It can be noted that most symmetrical female faces were found in the 15th century, while most symmetrical male faces occurred in the 18th century. After that, both genders rapidly became much more asymmetrically represented in all styles during the 19th and 20th centuries. From the 15th to the 18th century, representations of human faces seem to have moved within a stripe of relatively constant symmetry with maximums of symmetry around 0.35 and minimums of 0.32. This stripe of constant symmetry conforms to what we call the classical representation of the human face, which is the product of two factors: first, a cultural conception that placed the highest aesthetic valuation on previous models of beauty, specifically in the Greek and Roman models recovered during the Renaissance, and made their imitation and reproduction the goals of the artist; second, a training system based on workshops and academies that fostered an education around skills and models that helped achieve the former goals.[21] Variation within the classical mode can be attributed to the action-reaction effects that certain schools provoked against the previous dominant style, such as the separation from the ideal of symmetry proposed by Rococo artists versus more traditional styles such as Baroque and Neoclassicism.[22]

The appearance of disruptive styles in painting starting in the 19th century, a trend that became more acute throughout the 20th century when movements such as Modernism, Avant-Garde, Impressionism, Surrealism, Cubism, and Pop-Art dominated the art scene, came with a radical distancing from the ideal of symmetry in the representation of the human face. Paintings like Picasso's *Les Demoiselles d'Avignon*, Duchamp's *Nude Descending a Staircase, No. 2*, or Pollock's *Male and Female* responded to the new paradigms of human representation and to new approaches to beauty (Fig. 5).[23] This ultimately led to a poor detection of

Figure 4: Peak values of symmetry and averageness are found in the 15th and 18th centuries, decreasing slightly in between, but notably cresting in the extremes of the period (values of 1 indicate perfect symmetry, while 0 means total asymmetry). After the 18th century both values decrease equally until the 20th century, where we encounter the lowest average of symmetry and averageness of the last five centuries. Corresponding figures for specific painting styles for each century can be found in tables S1 to S5. (A) Average values of symmetry for the period between the 13th and 20th centuries, represented for male, female and both genders combined. (B) Average values of averageness for the same period for male and female compared to the corresponding composite and the composite of both genders.

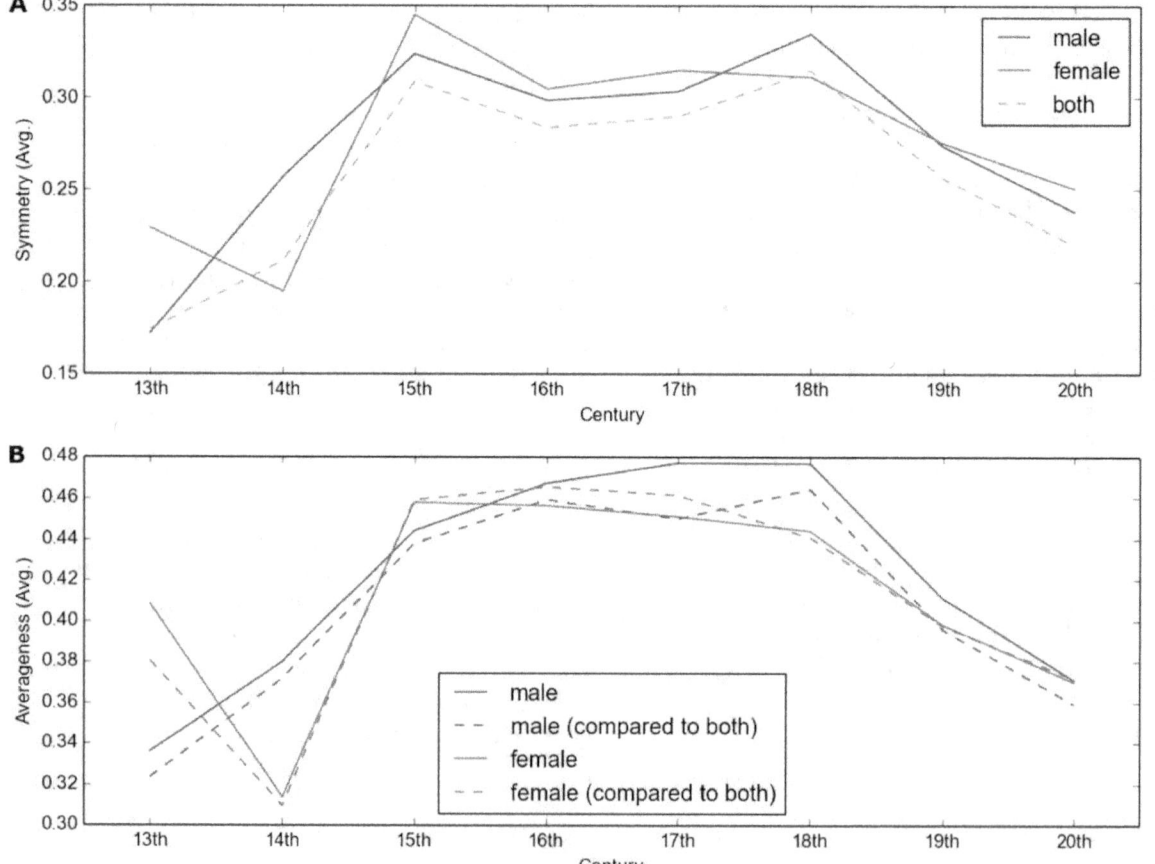

such faces by the algorithm, and therefore it explains why the averaged faces for the 20th century are still close to the picture-perfect representation of a human face (Fig. 2).

In the 20th century we also observe a considerable decrease (Fig. 6) in the ratio of faces detected in paintings as most of the aforementioned styles did not render realistic models of the human, rejected beauty, or simply tended to focus on concepts, dreams, or ideas in which the human being was not the central object.[24] This trend coincided with both the irruption of photography as the favorite medium to represent the human face and the movement of nonrepresentational art observed at the beginning of the same century and characterized as the "dehumanization of art."[25]

A consequence of these differences in symmetry is reflected in the oscillations in averageness throughout art history. Figure 4B showed the distribution of

Figure 5: New representations of the human face arose in the past century.
(A) Les Demoiselles d'Avignon by Pablo Picasso, 1907 (oil over canvas, 96 in × 92 in). Museum of Modern Art, New York. Image in the public domain ("Les Demoiselles d'Avignon," MOMA, accessed January 1, 2015, http://www.moma.org/explore/conservation/demoiselles/)
(B) Nu descendant un escalier n° 2 by Marcel Duchamp, 1912 (oil over canvas, 57 7/8 in × 35 1/8 in). Philadelphia Museum of Art, Philadelphia. Image in the public domain ("Nude Descending a Staircase (No. 2)," Philadelphia Museum of Art, accessed January 1, 2015, http://www.philamuseum.org/collections/permanent/51449.html)

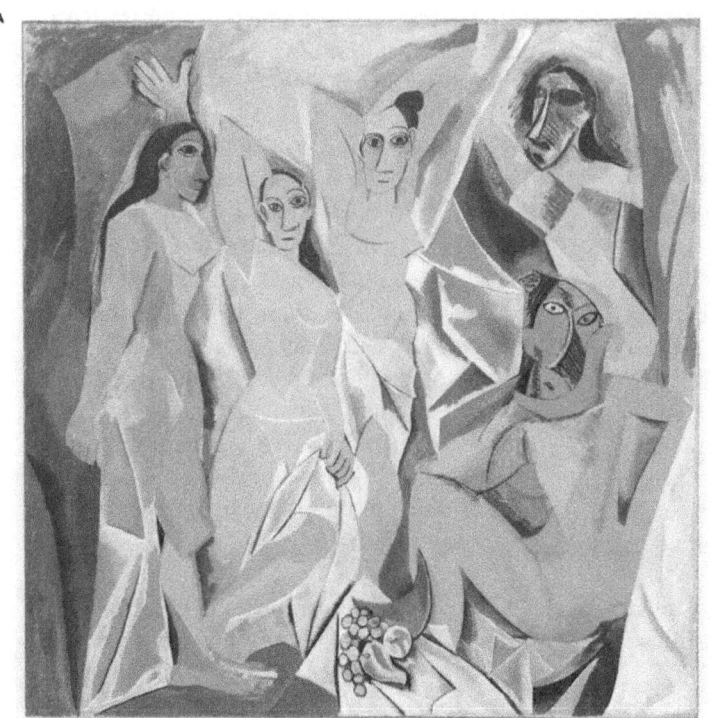
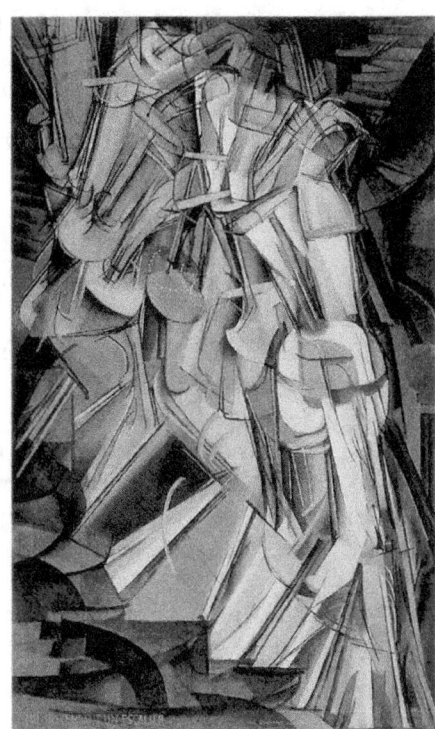

averageness for male and female faces compared to their gender-specific averaged composite. In dashed lines we can also see the same distribution but with regards to the average face generated from both genders. A two-sample Kolmogorov–Smirnov test allows us to see that there is no significant difference between the two male distributions ($p=0.92$) and the two female ones ($p=0.51$).

Averageness, the difference between a face and the averaged composite face of each century, can shed light on how similar faces are to each other. For male faces, we observe that the levels of averageness are low in the 13th century, but then begin to increase until the 17th century, when averageness of faces gradually decreases until the minimums recorded in 20th-century painting styles.

Culturomics of art history

Exact measurements such as averageness and symmetry help us better understand the various ways in which human faces have been depicted throughout the history of painting. However, as attested by art historians through traditional scholarship, these representations have not always remained constant, as different artistic styles have attempted their own ways of capturing facial beauty. After our analysis, we can conclude that there have been variations in the form in which facial beauty has been represented over time, and that these variations can be measured and tracked accurately. Of course, as in all data-based research endeavors, the better the dataset, the better the conclusions we can infer from our analysis. While there is a clear stripe conforming to features of classical representation of the human face from the 15th to the 18th centuries, both the 13th century –Gothic style– and contemporary art have shown clear deviations from the classical paradigm. Especially interesting is the data from 20th-century artistic styles, which shows low levels of both symmetry and averageness as well as a reduced proportion of total faces captured when compared with previous centuries.

These results conform to the views of art historians regarding the aesthetic and methodological disruptions that occurred after the vanguards. There has arguably been a change in the concept of art itself as well as in the theories that explain and criticize it. It is nowadays accepted that the representation of the human does not necessarily attempt to represent beauty. This shift in thought is clear in the data analysis and opens the door to a second phase of the investigation. By contrasting the aesthetic theories of specific periods and artists against the data, we would be able to establish their levels of conformity to and deviation from the objective measures of beauty. This would allow us to complement the qualitative and conceptual analysis of art history with the study of quantitative data. Combining these two levels appropriately should be one of the methodological aims of any culturomics science.

The separation from the classical mode of representing the human in contemporary art also serves as a reminder of the bias that we imposed on the analysis of perceived beauty by employing such accurate measuring systems. This bias also shows the interesting close relationship between classic ideas of beauty and art in Western cultures, and mathematical notions that support data-driven methods of research. While it is evident that the examples in Picasso's, Duchamp's, and Pollock's works show deviations from painting styles which depict faces that conform better to measures of symmetry and averageness, the judgment of whether these human faces are more or less beautiful than previous cases remains as aesthetic one. The contingency of aesthetic values is subject to fads, trends, reactions, and public opinion.[26]

Better algorithms can help us be more precise in the measurement of objective elements, although it has to be noted that the discipline that studies how social movements get started, become important and disappear, remains in its infancy.[27] Once we have improved the way to measure and analyze both the internal features of art works and the dynamics of social movements that create judgments about those works, we will be able to approach these types of problems in a more accurate manner.

Another relevant factor to take into account has to do with how representative the sampling used for this study is. While we are certain about the validity of the used set as related to art history, it is impossible to ascertain how representative these faces are of the real populations living in the various historical periods. However, we have observed that there is a correlation between the production of various types of media and the size of the human population in various

Figure 6: Number of paintings and faces per century, and ratio (faces per painting) between both.

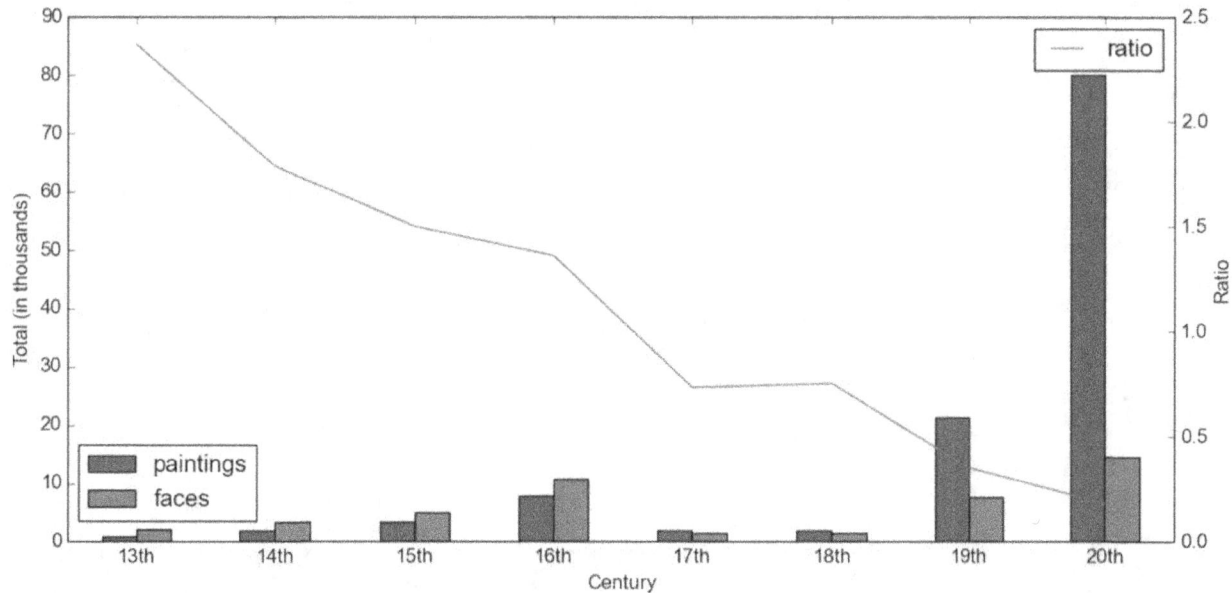

countries throughout time (Fig. 7, A and B). The more people, the more media is produced (*p*=1.02e-05 for books). This correlation remains true for paintings (*p*=3.92e-04, see figure 7C).

Although not explicitly discussed in this work, we have also verified that age, gender and face orientation, along with symmetry and averageness in the representation of human faces in paintings can become a complementary and objective way to identify and characterize styles and movements. Along with the exhaustive tagging for techniques, materials and the analysis and recording of chemical products used in art production, this could become the basis for the culturomics of art history.[28] Nevertheless, and although this does not contradict our findings, it is clear that there is also a variety of complex social, aesthetic and evolutionary elements that influence our judgment on beauty. Capturing these constructs into proper algorithms has not resulted yet in perfect solutions to ac-

Figure 7: Population growth and media production over time. (A) Book production as contained in WorldCat since year 1200. (B) Population growth of Europe, where most paintings are from, in the same period. (C) Paintings in our dataset.

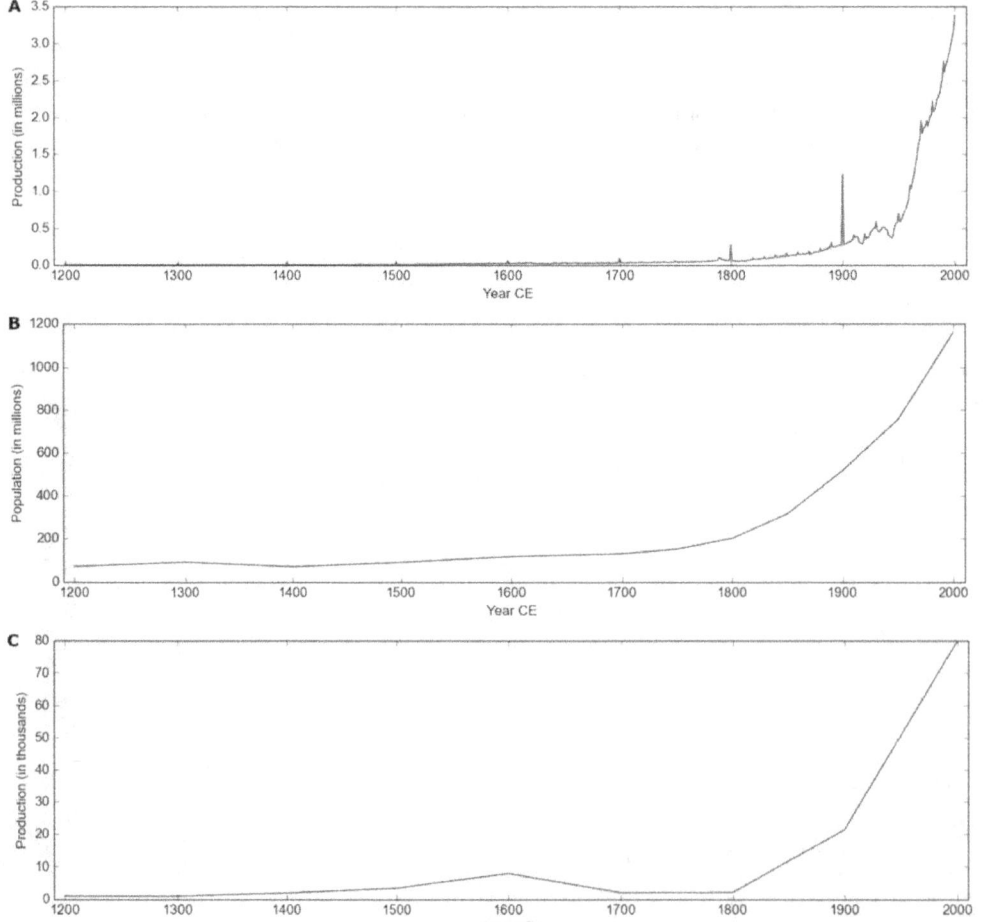

count for changes in perceived beauty. As we have previously stated, this has to do in part with the close relation between classic ideas and mathematical models that biased the analysis towards certain ideas of beauty. It is also important to note that many of these variations are due to the pressure that culture exerts in the short term on the adoption of different traits, and the deviations that this provokes from well-established, long term genetic features related to beauty, reproduction, and social acceptance and belonging.[29] Thus, it is important that any approach to the culturomics of art history and beauty also takes into account cultural evolution and cultural history as forces that shape the results we find in the data, and that have to contribute to the explanation of those results.

Supplementary Material

To this article supplementary material can be found at HeiDATA Dataverse Network http://dx.doi.org/10.11588/data/10057

Figures S1-5
Tables S1-5
External Database S1. List of paintings and metadata, paintings.xlsx
External Database S2. List of faces and features, faces.xlsx
External Database S3. List of authors and number of paintings, authors.xlsx

Notes

[1] Acknowledgments: We acknowledge the support of the Social Sciences and Humanities Research Council of Canada through a Major Collaborative Research Initiative. And the Canada Foundation for Innovation through the Leaders Opportunity Fund.

[2] Katie Kindelan, "Britain's 'Most Beautiful Face' Reveals Beauty Secrets," *abc News*, accessed January 1, 2014, http://abcnews.go.com/blogs/lifestyle/2012/04/britains-most-beautiful-face-reveals-beauty-secrets/.

[3] Grammer, Karl, and Randy Thornhill. "Human (*Homo sapiens*) facial attractiveness and sexual selection: the role of symmetry and averageness." *Journal of comparative psychology* 108.3 (1994): 233.

[4] William Hogarth, Ed., *The Analysis of Beauty* (Heidelberg Univ., http://archiv.ub.uni-heidelberg.de/artdok/volltexte/2010/1217/, 2010).

[5] Rowland, Ingrid D., and Thomas Noble Howe, eds. *Vitruvius: 'Ten Books on Architecture'* (Cambridge: Cambridge University Press, 1999).

[6] Nancy Etcoff, *Survival of the prettiest: The science of beauty* (Random House Digital, 2011).

[7] Francis Galton, ed., *Inquiries into human faculty and its development* (Kessinger Publishing, 2010).

[8] See the foundational works by Randy Thornhill, and Steven W. Gangestad. "Facial attractiveness." *Trends in cognitive sciences* 3, no. 12 (1999): 452-460; Barber, Nigel. "The evolutionary psychology of physical attractiveness: Sexual selection and human morphology." *Ethology and Sociobiology* 16, no. 5 (1995): 395-424; W. Yu Douglas, and Glenn H. Shepard. "Is beauty in the eye of the beholder?." *Nature* 396, no. 6709 (1998): 321-322; and David I. Perrett *et al.*, "Effects of sexual dimorphism on facial attractiveness." *Nature* 394, no. 6696 (1998): 884-887.

[9] Paul R. Abramson, and Steven D. Pinkerton, eds. *Sexual nature/sexual culture* (Chicago: University of Chicago Press, 1995); David M. Buss, "Sex differences in human mate preferences: Evolutionary hypotheses tested in 37 cultures." *Behavioral and brain sciences* 12, no. 01 (1989): 1-14.; Michael R. Cunningham *et al.*, "Their ideas of beauty are, on the whole, the same as ours." Consistency and variability in the cross-cultural perception of female physical attractiveness. *J. Pers. Soc. Psychol* 68 (1995): 261-279.; Doug Jones, and Kim Hill. "Criteria of facial attractiveness in five populations." *Human Nature* 4, no. 3 (1993): 271-296; and Diane S. Berry, "Attractiveness, attraction, and sexual selection: Evolutionary perspectives on the form and function of physical attractiveness." *Advances in experimental social psychology* 32 (2000): 273-342.

[10] Bernhard Fink, and Ian Penton-Voak, "Evolutionary psychology of facial attractiveness," *Current Directions in Psychological Science* 11, no. 5 (2002): 154-158; Karen Dion, Ellen Berscheid, and Elaine Walster. "What is beautiful is good," *Journal of personality and social psychology* 24, no. 3 (1972): 285.

[11] Gillian Rhodes, and Leslie A. Zebrowitz, *Facial attractiveness: Evolutionary, cognitive, and social perspectives* (New Jersey: Ablex Publishing Corporation, 2002), 1.

[12] Judith H. Langlois, and Lori A. Roggman, "Attractive faces are only average," *Psychological science* 1, no. 2 (1990): 115-121.

[13] See Lev Manovich's "Selfiecity", accessed January 1, 2015, http://selfiecity.net/; and "One Hundred Million Creative Commons Flickr Images for Research," *Yahoo! Labs*, accessed January 1, 2015, http://yahoolabs.tumblr.com/post/89783581601/one-hundred-million-creative-commons-flickr-images-for.

[14] "Ciudad de la Pintura," accessed November 1, 2013, http://pintura.aut.org/.

[15] "WikiArt, Virtual Art Encyclopedia," accessed January 1, 2015, http://www.wikiart.org/.

[16] Summary tables of the dataset are shown in tables S1 to S4 and figures S2 to S5 in the section Supplementary Materials (SM).

[17] We used the service faces.com before it was purchased and shut down by Facebook in 2012. "Facebook to buy facial-recognition startup: sources" *Reuter*, accessed January 1, 2015, http://uk.reuters.com/article/2012/06/18/us-facebook-face-idUKBRE85H1A320120618.

[18] Grammer and Thornhill, *Homo sapiens*.

[19] A reference implementation of these formulas can be found in "Your Face in History," accessed January 1, 2015, http://faces.cultureplex.ca/, a website that gives the user the chance to take a picture of herself and compare the obtained symmetry index with the symmetry of the faces included in this study and see, therefore, for which century her face would better work.

[20] Gillian Rhodes, "The evolutionary psychology of facial beauty," *Annu. Rev. Psychol.* 57 (2006): 199-226.

[21] See Karl F. Morrison, *The Mimetic Tradition of Reform in the West* (Princeton: Princeton Univ. Press, Princeton, 1982); Gunter Gebauer, and Christoph Wulf, *Mimesis: Culture, Art, and Society* (Berkeley: Univ. of California Press, 1995); Kenneth Gouwens, "Perceiving the Past: Renaissance Humanism after the "Cognitive Turn"," *American Historical Review* 55–82 (1998); Bernard Weinberg, *A History of Literary Criticism in the Italian Renaissance*, Vol. 1 (Chicago: Chicago Univ. Press, 1961); and Paul O. Kristeller, *The classics and Renaissance Thought*, Vol. 15 (Chicago: Harvard Univ. Press, 1955).

[22] Ernst H. Gombrich, *The Story of Art*, Vol. 15 (London: Phaidon, 1995).

[23] For Pollock's Male and Female, see "Male and Female," Philadelphia Museum of Art, accessed January 1, 2015, http://www.philamuseum.org/collections/permanent/69527.html.

[24] Wendy Steiner, *Venus in exile: the rejection of beauty in twentieth-century art* (Chicago: Univ. of Chicago Press, 2002); Umberto Eco, and Alastair McEwen, *History of Beauty* (New York: Rizzoli, 2004).

[25] José Ortega y Gasset, *The Dehumanization of Art and Other Essays on Art, Culture, and Literature* (Princeton: Princeton Univ. Press, 1968).

[26] Denis Dutton, *The art instinct: beauty, pleasure, & human evolution* (Oxford: Oxford Univ. Press, 2009).

[27] Alex Pentland, *Social Physics: How Good Ideas Spread–The Lessons from a New Science* (New York: Penguin Press, 2014).

[28] Jean-Baptiste Michel et al., Quantitative analysis of culture using millions of digitized books, *Science* 331.6014, 176–182 (2011).

[29] Juan Luis Suárez, Fernando Sancho, and Javier de la Rosa, "Sustaining a global community: Art and religion in the network of baroque hispanic-american paintings," *Leonardo* 45, no. 3 (2012): 281-281.

Bibliography

ABC News. "Britain's 'Most Beautiful Face' Reveals Beauty Secrets." Accessed July 1, 2014. http://abcnews.go.com/blogs/lifestyle/2012/04/britains-most-beautiful-face-reveals-beauty-secrets/.

Barber, Nigel. "The evolutionary psychology of physical attractiveness: Sexual selection and human morphology." *Ethology and Sociobiology* 16.5 (1995): 395–424.

Berry, Diane S. "Attractiveness, attraction, and sexual selection: Evolutionary perspectives on the form and function of physical attractiveness." *Advances in experimental social psychology* 32 (2000): 273-342.

Biraben, Jean Noël. "An essay concerning mankind's demographic evolution." *Journal of Human Evolution* 9, no. 8 (1980): 655-663.

Bos, Eduard, My T. Vu, Ann Levin, and Rodolfo A. Bulatao, in *Estimates and Projections with Related Demographic Statistics*, Vol. 8, pp 515. Baltimore: The World Bank and Johns Hopkins Press, 1993.

Buss, David M. "Sex differences in human mate preferences: Evolutionary hypotheses tested in 37 cultures." *Behavioral and brain sciences* 12.1 (1989): 1-14.

Ciudad de la Pintura. Accessed November 1, 2012. http://pintura.aut.org/.

Clark, Colin. *Population growth and land use*. New York: MacMillan, 1967.

CulturePlex. "Your Face in History" Accessed October 1, 2014. http://faces.cultureplex.ca/.

Cunningham, Michael R., Alan R. Roberts, Anita P. Barbee, Perri B. Druen, and Cheng-Huan Wu. "" Their ideas of beauty are, on the whole, the same as ours": Consistency and variability in the cross-cultural perception of female physical attractiveness." *Journal of Personality and Social Psychology* 68. 2 (1995): 261-279.

Dion, Karen, Ellen Berscheid, and Elaine Walster. "What is beautiful is good." *Journal of personality and social psychology* 24.3 (1972): 285-290.

Durand, John. D. "Historical estimates of world population: An evaluation." *Population and Development Review* (1977): 253-296.

Dutton, Denis. *The art instinct: beauty, pleasure, & human evolution*. Oxford: Oxford University Press, 2009.

Eco, Umberto, and Alastair McEwen. "History of beauty." New York: Rizzoli, 2005.

Etcoff, Nancy. *Survival of the prettiest: The science of beauty*. Random House Digital, 2011.

Fink, Bernhard, and Ian Penton-Voak. "Evolutionary Psychology of Facial Attractiveness." *Current Directions in Psychological Science* 11 (2002): 154–158.

Galton, F., Ed., *Inquiries into human faculty and its development*. Kessinger Publishing, 2010.

Gebauer, Gunter, and Christoph Wulf. *Mimesis: culture, art, society*. Berkeley: University of California Press, 1995.

Gombrich, Ernst Hans. *The story of art*. Vol. 15. London: Phaidon, 1995.

Gouwens, Kenneth. "Perceiving the Past: Renaissance Humanism after the 'Cognitive Turn'." *American Historical Review* (1998): 55-82.

Grammer, Karl, and Randy Thornhill. "Human (Homo sapiens) facial attractiveness and sexual selection: the role of symmetry and averageness." *Journal of comparative psychology* 108.3 (1994): 233.

Haub, Carl. *2005 World Population Data Sheet*. Washington, DC: Population Reference Bureau, 2005.

---. *2006 World Population Data Sheet*. Washington, DC: Population Reference Bureau, 2006.

---. *2007 World Population Data Sheet*. Washington, DC: Population Reference Bureau, 2007.

---. *2008 World Population Data Sheet*. Washington, DC: Population Reference Bureau, 2008.

Hogarth, William., Ed., *The Analysis of Beauty* (Heidelberg Univ., http://archiv.ub.uni-heidelberg.de/artdok/voll texte/2010/1217/, 2010).

International Data Base (IDB), *U.S. Census Bureau*. Accessed November 2014. www.census.gov/population/international/data/idb/informationGateway.php.

Jones, Doug, and Kim Hill. "Criteria of facial attractiveness in five populations." *Human Nature* 4, no. 3 (1993): 271-296.

Klein Goldewijk, K., G. van Drecht, in *Integrated Modelling of Global Environmental Change*, , pp. 93–112, A. F. Bouwman, T. Kram, K. Klein Goldewijk, Eds. Bilthoven: Netherlands Environmental Assessment Agency (MNP), 2006.

Kristeller, Paul Oskar. *The classics and Renaissance Thought.* Chicago: Harvard University Press, 1955.

Langlois, Judith H., and Lori A. Roggman. "Attractive faces are only average." *Psychological science* 1.2 (1990): 115-121.

Maddison, Angus. "The world economy. volume 2: Historical statistics." Paris: Development Centre Studies, Organisation for Economic Co-operation and Development (OECD), 2006.

McEvedy, Colin, and Richard Jones. *Atlas of world population history.* Harmondsworth: Penguin, 1978.

Michel, Jean-Baptiste, Yuan Kui Shen, Aviva Presser Aiden, Adrian Veres, Matthew K. Gray, Joseph P. Pickett, Dale Hoiberg et al. "Quantitative analysis of culture using millions of digitized books." *Science* 331.6014 (2011): 176-182.

MOMA. "Les Demoiselles d'Avignon". Accessed July 1, 2014. http://www.moma.org/explore/conservation/demoiselles/.

Morrison, Karl F. *The mimetic tradition of reform in the West.* Princeton: Princeton University Press, 1982.

Ortega y Gasset, José. *The dehumanization of art: and other essays on art, culture, and literature.* Vol. 128. Princeton: Princeton University Press, 1968.

Pentland, Alex. *Social Physics: How Good Ideas Spread-The Lessons from a New Science.* New York: Penguin, 2014.

Perrett, D. I., K. J. Lee, I. Penton-Voak, D. Rowland, S. Yoshikawa, D. M. Burt, S. P. Henzi, D. L. Castles, and S. Akamatsu. "Effects of sexual dimorphism on facial attractiveness." *Nature* 394.6696 (1998): 884-887.

Philadelphia Museum of Art. "Male and Female". Accessed July 1, 2014. http://www.philamuseum.org/ collections/permanent/69527.html.

---. "Nude Descending a Staircase (No. 2)" Accessed July 1, 2014. http://www.philamuseum.org/collections/permanent/51449.html.

Rhodes, Gillian, and Leslie A. Zebrowitz. *Facial attractiveness: Evolutionary, cognitive, and social perspectives.* Norwood: Ablex Publishing Corporation, 2002.

– Advertisement –

Rhodes, Gillian. "The evolutionary psychology of facial beauty." *Annu. Rev. Psychol.* 57 (2006): 199-226.

Rowland, Ingrid D., and Thomas Noble Howe, eds. *Vitruvius:'Ten Books on Architecture'*. Cambridge: Cambridge University Press, 1999.

Schich, Maximilian, Chaoming Song, Yong-Yeol Ahn, Alexander Mirsky, Mauro Martino, Albert-László Barabási, and Dirk Helbing. "A network framework of cultural history." *Science* 345.6196 (2014): 558-562.

Steiner, Wendy. *Venus in Exile: The Rejection of Beauty in Twentieth-Century Art.* Chicago: University of Chicago Press, 2002.

Suárez, Juan Luis, Fernando Sancho, and Javier de la Rosa. "Sustaining a global community: Art and religion in the network of baroque hispanicamerican paintings." *Leonardo* 45.3 (2012): 281-281.

Abramson, Paul R., and Steven D. Pinkerton, eds. Sexual nature/sexual culture. University of Chicago Press, 1995.

Tanton, John H. "End of the migration epoch." *The Social Contract* 4.3 (1994): 162-173.

Tifentale, Alise, and Lev Manovich. "Selfiecity: Exploring Photography and Self-Fashioning in Social Media." Accessed January 1, 2015. http://selfiecity.net/

Thomlinson, Ralph. *Demographic Problems: Controversy over population control.* Belmont: Dickenson Publishing Company, 1975.

Thornhill, Randy, and Steven W. Gangestad. "Facial attractiveness." *Trends in cognitive sciences* 3.12 (1999): 452-460.

United Nations Department of Economic and Social Affairs Estimates (ESA), "The World at Six Billion" (United Nations, New York, 1999).

---, *World Population Prospects: The 2008 Revision* (United Nations, New York, 2009).

United States Census Bureau. "World population: Historical estimates of world population" Accessed October 1, 2014. www.census.gov/population/international/data/worldpop/table_history.php.

Weinberg, Bernard. *A history of literary criticism in the Italian Renaissance.* Vol. 2. Chicago: University of Chicago Press, 1961.

WikiArt, Virtual Art Encyclopedia. Accessed October 1, 2014. http://www.wikiart.org/.

Wikipedia "World population estimates." Accessed October 1, 2014. http://en.wikipedia.org/w/index.php?title=World_population_estimates&oldid=626906164.

Yahoo! Labs. "One Hundred Million Creative Commons Flickr Images for Research" Accessed July 1, 2014. http://yahoolabs.tumblr.com/post/89783581601/one-hundred-million-creative-commons-flickr-images-for.

Yu, Douglas W., and Glenn H. Shepard. "Is beauty in the eye of the beholder?" *Nature* 396.6709 (1998): 321-322.

Javier de la Rosa Javier de la Rosa is Ph.D. Candidate in Hispanic Studies and Tech Lead and Developer Chief at the CulturePlex Lab at the University of Western Ontario. As an Engineer and Computer Scientist he has a solid background in Artificial Intelligence and Machine Learning (B.Sc. and M.S.), disciplines that he loves to apply to his new field of research on Digital Humanities, where he combines his two most preferred passions.

Correspondence e-mail: versae@gmail.com

Juan-Luis Suárez is a Professor in the Modern Languages and Literatures Department and the Director of the CulturePlex Lab at the University of Western Ontario. His research deals with culturomics, cultural history, cultural complexity and complexity theory, lean big data, the evolution of the Baroque, technologies of humanism, entrepreneurship, as well as globalization. He also spearheaded a successful IDI proposal at in the field of Digital Humanities on which he is collaborating with participants from a broad spectrum of fields of study.

Call for Manuscripts #2: Visualizing Big Image Data

Art History is based on empirical research. We gain knowledge using visual data. Precise observation, comparison and classification of objects of art are the fundamentals of our discipline. With the rise of Digital Art History, this process has become digitized.

Digital Art History means using the computer to support researchers with their epistemic goals. The computer can process more images than a human can look at in a lifetime. Hence, visual information has to be collected and processed, made accessible and analyzed. The analysis of Big Image Data is a great opportunity for Art History and adds new methods to the discipline.

Today, art historians are not only interpreting pictures but becoming picture-makers themselves. Large amounts of image data can only be analyzed through visualizations. These images are themselves in need of interpretation. Clearly, this falls into the domain of art history.

The second issue of the DAH-Journal will focus on "Visualizing Big Image Data". Data visualizations raise new questions and we welcome articles which are discussing questions surrounding this topic, e.g.: How to interpret such images? How do visualizations generate new insights? How is order established by means of pictures today? What is the relation of a quantitative research to qualitative research – and what does this actually mean in art history? What data do we need to acquire in the first place? And what are the best visualization tools currently available for art historical research?

The topic of visualizations also raises questions of how the interdisciplinary exchange between art historians and computer scientists works and how it should develop in the future. To what extent are art historians dependent on computer scientists in order to generate and effectively use the possibilities of digital metapictures? Is there a case for closer collaborations and/or do art historians need to fill the gaps in their knowledge of digital technology?

The second issue of the DAH-Journal is scheduled for end of 2015. Featured author will be Maximilian Schich. He is an Associate Professor in Arts and Technology and a founding member of the Edith O'Donnell Institute for Art History at the University of Texas at Dallas.

In order to hand in manuscripts, authors need to register at http://dah-journal.org/register.html by **August, 30 2015** (6000 words max.). For more information for authors, please visit "Information for Authors" on our website http://www.dah-journal.org/authors.html

http://dah-journal.org

www.ingramcontent.com/pod-product-compliance
Lightning Source LLC
Chambersburg PA
CBHW082207220526
45470CB00010B/3072